Oded Ezer

The Typographer's Guide to the Galaxy

gestalten

Oded Ezer
The Typographer's
Guide to the Galaxy

TABLE OF CONTENT

Preface

Fonts

Graphic Work

Between the Letters

Experimental Work

Index

Imprint

Oded Ezer
The Typographer's
Guide to the Galaxy

Foreword by <u>Paola Antonelli</u>

HAVE YOU EVER LOOKED AT YOUR HANDWRITING FROM THE OTHER SIDE OF THE SHEET, HOLDING THE PAPER AGAINST THE LIGHT?

∞ It is as displacing as watching your own photographic portrait and realizing that all the asymmetries you thought you knew and accepted are back in full force, making you look really odd and twisted and revealing a new soul. In the case of type and writing, it is a litmus test. There is no better proof of the elegance of a typeface than obfuscating its content. And if, as is my case when it comes to Hebrew (or Korean, or Thai, or Arabic...), one does not understand anything at all, there is no need to even reverse the sheet; the experience becomes purely emotional and aesthetic. Ah, the delights of ignorance! Characters from different alphabets become fantastic creatures and take on lives of their own. In the case of Oded Ezer, who calls himself a "typographic experimentalist," some letters are indeed endowed with DNA and a biological structure, and become crawling insects and sperm.

I first encountered Oded Ezer's work while I was doing research for my exhibition Design and the Elastic Mind, which opened at The Museum of Modern Art at the beginning of 2008. The exhibition focused on some designers' ability to interpret scientific and technological revolutions and transform them into objects that people can use – in other words to transform revolutions into real life. It was a show about experimental design and about the relationship between design and science, so I cannot express enough my elation when I saw Oded Ezer, a communication designer, appear on his website wearing a white lab coat and contemplating a vial, surrounded by tools that have nothing to do with those found in a typical design office.

For the exhibition I chose one project, Typosperma, which is part of Oded's series Biotypography. The subject of the fictional experiment are cloned spermatozoa with typographic information implanted into their DNA, "some sort of new transgenic creatures, half (human) sperm, half letter." Typosperma made me think of many endlessly fascinating consequences – from the name of a new baby being decided at the moment of conception, to the idea that each ejaculation could be a uniquely original and lyrical poem. In the exhibition galleries, Typosperma was featured next to Lithoparticles, the work of two bona fide scientists, Thomas Mason and Carlos Fernandez, biochemists from the University of California, Los Angeles, who had invented a new way to mark proteins using nano-scale letters. The meeting between the two scientists and Oded is a moment I will never forget because in the excitement, curiosity, and admiration they all had for each other lies the future direction not only of design, but also of science. They will not only need, but also seek out, an alliance to dream bigger and experiment.

Typeface design is a very rigorous, almost scientific discipline where minuscule variations and adaptations reverberate in meaning and impact. The formula for a successful typeface is the result of an enormous amount of trial-and-error work, not unlike a scientific experiment. Like scientists, typeface designers sometimes need to blow some steam. Ezer in particular felt the need to escape not only the exactitude of type design, but also the obsessive goal-orientation typical of the Israeli educational system. That is how he came to live a double life, as a successful commercial designer on one hand and as a pilgrim on a "path to the unknown," as he calls it, on the other.

Before Oded decided to mix chemistry and typography, his work already explored the inner soul of letters by letting them channel the personality of a poet's or a musician's work. He let them become three-dimensional and animated in posters and book covers –a direction explored across the centuries by armies of type designers, declared or unaware, and reprised by Ezer with renewed elegance. In a project called Tortured Letters, he bound, gagged, and stretched single Latin and Hebrew characters with frightening sadism. In another, he moulded them to look like little ants, already on the path to being full-fledged organisms. The Biotypography project in particular holds great promise for the future. Ezer thinks that since, very often, a type designer chooses a typeface for its ability to embody and render the feeling of a project, the step from object to creature is direct and typefaces should really become living, biological beings. As he explains it, "The term Biotypography refers to any application that uses biological systems, living organisms, or derivatives thereof to create or modify typographical phenomena." These fantastical creatures not only literally embody the dream of design and science coming together, but also let us dream about a super-human language that is shaped by biology, rather than by culture –the dream of a universal means of communication that we have sought for centuries.

Paola Antonelli is Senior Curator in the Department of Architecture and Design at the Museum of Modern Art, New York.

Oded Ezer
The Typographer's Guide to the Galaxy

Foreword by Marian Bantjes

ODED EZER NAGGED AT MY CONSCIOUSNESS FOR A COUPLE OF YEARS BEFORE I MET HIM. I HAD SEEN HIS WORK AND RECOGNIZED ITS BREATHTAKING BRILLIANCE AND, I CONFESS, I WAS JEALOUS ENOUGH TO HOPE THAT THIS MAN MIGHT BE A ONE-TRICK PONY. ALAS AND HURRAY, HE WAS AND IS NOT.

∞ Oded's ability to view the letterform as a 3-dimensional object has led him to startling exercises in experimental form. But at the same time, by working largely by hand, he has been able to explore the form in a much more inventive way than we have commonly seen by those who work in artificial 3D environments. His physical handling of the letterforms reveals both a tenacity and delicacy, as though he were spinning glass, pounding metal into foil, or throwing pizza dough. There is give and stretch, but no breakage in his deliberate manipulation. It looks like fun, but the beauty of the results assures us that it is work.

Call this a trick, if you must, but Oded has employed it in enough ways to variable effect that he is able to turn the trick into magic. He makes the inanimate animate: words stand and wave, spill their guts, then take a bow. In fact, as one who often has difficulty describing myself, I think perhaps the best way to describe Oded is as typographic animator. Despite the stillness of the image, his work is so active, and the characters so alive, it's hard not to imagine them getting up and walking. Which, of course, they do in several instances.

The Biotypography project seems to be the point at which all those waving, straining letterforms finally achieve their freedom, grow legs and venture forth. Now incarnate as insectoidal, letters take their mutant forms to the road. None of them seem quite anatomically correct; they have too many legs, or not enough, and appendages where there should be none. It is all worrisome enough to keep us from opening a book at night.

One wonders, in fact, about Oded's taste in films: I suspect a library full of Sci-fi and horror. Predating the Biotypography Project by a few years, Oded's letterforms were already walking in a wobbly, twisted manner that speaks to their origin as prototypes from the laboratory: the Plastica poster figures are just barely alive – these constructed zombies would be menacing but for the fact that they still seem to be learning to put one foot before the next. I suspect that, like Daleks[1], they cannot handle stairs.

Thus, having so far compared Oded Ezer to a magician and an animator, with some allusion to the occult, I am imagining him now as all of the above: perhaps as The Reanimator[2] – in short, a mad scientist. In fact, yes, I think the picture of him on the back cover from The Rooms project shows this perfectly as he daringly allows one of his wiggling letters to climb on his head! From the same project we can see some of his more abortive early experiments where, like in the early trials of the machine from The Fly[3] the letters seem to have had some kind of nasty accident which has exposed and scrambled their viscera. But like any good mad scientist, Oded is not only always willing to try again, but ready with some new twist or technique. The images on page 112 show him formulating some kind of suspicious green gel as he takes his typography to the cellular level with his work on Typosperma. No more the reliance on incisions by knife, or transmutation by clumsy mechanical inventions; typography now swims in our bodies and changes the very possibility of humanity itself. With all this in mind, perhaps the less inferred about the Tortured Letters project the better!

Well, enough! I fear I have painted poor Oded as a diabolical madman, infecting typography with a kind of cross-eyed sickness, and this just could not be further from the truth. He may or may not spend too much time watching strange movies, but mostly he is inventive and full of humour. The results of his feverish work are not only compellingly quirky, they are most often extremely beautiful. There is, to my knowledge, no one else doing work like this, and I am grateful to know such a pioneer.

I have met Oded Ezer only once. Despite my almost crippling jealousy, I was excited to learn that we were both speaking at TypoBerlin in 2008. We had one of those moments of two people who had been watching each other from afar, tentatively and then enthusiastically meeting with mutual compliments and assertions of self-inferiority. Much to my relief, I discovered that Oded is actually a really nice guy and not at all insane. There is nothing to fear, and much to look forward to from this amazing manipulator of form; this typographic animator; this mad genius. Stay tuned.

Marian Bantjes (AGI), is a Canadian designer, artist, illustrator, typographer and writer.

1 **Daleks** are a clumsy and hysterical mutant "life" form introduced in 1963 in the TV series "Dr. Who."

2 **The Re-Animator** is a 1985 cult horror film about a medical student working on a formula to revive the dead, to various gruesome but oddly amusing results.

3 **The Fly** is a Sci-fi/horror film directed by David Cronenberg in 1986, based on a 1958 original. In it, the prototype for a teleportation device has an unfortunate habit of rematerialising organic beings inside out or fused together.

Fonts
Evolution vs. Revolution

by <u>Yehuda Hofshi</u>

ONE MORNING, RECENTLY, WHILE ON MY WAY TO A PRINTER IN TEL AVIV, MY EYES CAUGHT A GLIMPSE OF AN ABANDONED ONE-STORY BUILDING. I ENTERED, OUT OF CURIOSITY. IT WAS A USUAL TEL AVIV MORNING, WITH NOISY BUSES RUNNING, POMEGRANATE VENDORS ON THE CORNER; NEARBY, A STAND SELLING FAKE COMPACT DISCS AND AN OLD SEWING-APPLIANCES STORE BARELY MANAGE TO SURVIVE. FIG TREES DROP THEIR FRUIT, CREATING A STICKY, THICK LAYER ON THE SIDEWALK. IN FRONT OF A CLOSED BRANCH OF A BANK, A NEW SIGN READ LIMA LIMA MEMBERS CLUB, WHILE NEWSPAPER HEADLINES HUNG FROM ELECTRICITY WIRES FOR DAYS ON END.

fig 1: <u>1940's 'Shavit' can of instant coffee</u>

אבגדהוז
אבגדהוז
אבגדהו
אבגדההוז

fig 2: From top to bottom:
'Shoken' by Francesca Baruch, 'Koren' by Eliahu Koren,
'Hatzvi' by Zvi Housmann, 'Narkiss Classic' by Zvi Narkiss

אבגדהוז
אבגדדהוז
אבגדהו
אבגדהו
אבגדהו
אבגדהו
אבגדהו

fig 3: From top to bottom:
'Frank-Rühl' by Raphael Frank, 'Hadassah' by Henry
Friedlander, 'Haim' by Haim LeWit, 'Oron' by Asher Oron,
'Fudi' by Yanek Iontef, 'Alchemist' and 'Taagid'
by Oded Ezer

∞ I peered inside, trying to detect something I sensed waited for me hidden in the dephts of the rooms. There were empty vodka bottles strewn on the Art Noveau tiles, crumpled Red Bull cans and a pile of cigarette butts. I saw the dead body of a pigeon; a layer of sooty dust covered it all with a veil of mystery. A big wooden closet stood in the corner of one of the rooms. I approached it, not sure whether I should be wandering about this place. As I opened the closet, an exciting surprise awaited me there: on one of the shelves lay an old can of instant coffee with the original label still glued to it. The brand name was Shavit and the "logo" and cup of coffee underneath it had been drawn by hand, apparently in the 40's [fig 1]. When I looked more closely at the logo, I was taken aback by the style of the letters, which I had never seen before, as well as the naïve choice not to use an existing font, but rather to draw the letters especially for that product. The innocence in this endeavour and the non-pretentious form of the letters reflected a creative freedom and a lack of marketing awareness, much like an impressive drawing by a child who is not aware of what his hands have created.

In my numerous wanderings around Tel Aviv, where I live and work, I often uncover footprints of letters from signs designed for businesses in years long gone, names of buildings, numbers of houses as well as faded letters on synagogue windows and the like, all of them archaeological remnants of the modern age. Do they fascinate me solely due to the romantic nostalgia they bring of a period I did not even live through or is it perhaps a longing for the simple, the innocent and the personal, so rare in present times? This fascinating typographic playground, open to all, where game rules do not exist as of yet, enabled typographic creativity to spring. I saw this in the alluring can of instant coffee. The authenticity in its letters can also in similar objects emphasize the endless possibilities hidden in letter design. Although perceived by many as an elitist field, strict and somewhat cold, images at times familiar or anonymous are intense sources of inspiration to several contemporary designers who often ask themselves where, if at all, exists a border between the "permitted" and the "forbidden" – or, for that matter, between the accessible, the legible and the playful, and the uncommitted. Oded Ezer is one of the distinguished active contemporary designers in Israel whose work is characterized mainly by the special integration of the experimental and the practical. He joins his colleagues in the typographic "playground," although following different rules and with much more complex instruments, with the same fresh and exciting scent we sense in creations from the past.

EVOLUTION AND REVOLUTION

The evolution of the Hebrew letter in modern times was made possible thanks largely to font designers' persistent attempts over the years to change and improve the form of Hebrew letters. Some of the modern font designers chose to create a dialog with previous centuries. Others started from scratch and succeeded at inventing new and revolutionary styles in the form of the letter.

These two approaches are in fact a response to a new reality that emerged in a short period of time, starting at the end of the 19th century with the strengthening of Jewish national consciousness. The need for a definition of a Jewish national identity grew with the waves of Jewish immigrants who arrived in Israel on the eve of World War II. During and after the war, among the thousands of refugees who arrived in Israel, were letter designers whose creations were part of a national visual identity that was coming into being. The design of new Hebrew fonts met the practical need of local economic life, commerce and of secular cultural life that started to flourish in big cities like Jerusalem, Tel Aviv and Haifa. Designers such as Francesca Baruch, Moshe Spitzer, Eliahu Koren and Zvi Narkiss [fig.2] represent, in their attitude, an evolutionary approach that advocates a continuity in the form of the Hebrew letter over hundreds of years. In this approach, they tie the cultural and traditional past of the letter to the reality being shaped in the 20th century, up to the present. Parallel to them, designers such as Raphael Frank, Henry Friedlander, Haim LeWit, Asher Oron, Yanek Yontef, Oded Ezer and others [fig.3] chose a path that was perceived, in a certain sense, as essentially different. They preferred to attempt to create a logic of form, not influenced by historical typographic traditions but based on creativity and individualism. Still, in their work they did not deny the great responsibility to remain loyal to the principles of the written Hebrew language and its regularity. The extent to which they acted freely, broke conventions, experimented and were adventurous, differed from one person to the other, depending on their personality and the period in which they worked. Raphael Frank was the first to bring about a conceptual reform in the shape of the traditional Hebrew letter. Today it would be difficult for us to relate to his work as revolutionary or even as experimental. However, the Frank Rühl font, which was presented to the public in the early years of the 20th century, was received with much suspicion and reservation. It was perceived as breaking conventions, denying the sanctity of the Hebrew letter and as such was unacceptable. The writing rules of the Hebrew letters show close ties between form and religion. These rules appear in the text "Shulchan Aruch," which was the central source to be relied on in everything concerning the structure and form of the letter. Nevertheless, from the realization that it was necessary to make significant corrections to the form of the letter to conform to the spirit of the times, substantial changes were introduced by Frank for the first time ever. Letters such as yod, shin, ayin, tzadik and final tzadik, whose extremities were usually written with a slight slant until then, were now straightened and became parallel to the letter base. This testifies to a non compliance with calligraphy as the sole factor in the structure of the letter. The differences in line width in the vertical and horizontal lines of the letter were diminished, also as part of a distancing from the calligraphic aspect of the letter[fig.4]. In the letter peh, a white geometric shape which had not existed before became the marked sign of identification for the font over the years. Frank Rühl has since become the preferred and leading font in the press, journals and in books.

The Frankrühliah project by Oded Ezer is a hypothetical dialogue and a tribute to the work of Raphael Frank, timed to coincide with Frank Rühl's 100th anniversary. Oded Ezer's choice to address this specific font, instead of others, is not to be taken for granted. Its wide circulation and monopoly on the one hand, and the impressive attempts by font designers to create a font that equalled its success, on the other, has prevented others from competing or interfering with this, the "king" of fonts. Ezer's choice is typical of his personality: "Let's take the most sacred myth and work with it as a precious raw material, even if only for experimentation's sake." And at first, the project was defined as non-practical. The leading idea was to emphasize the Jugendstil characteristics of the original letter, albeit with a neo-Jugendstil approach. That is to say, he would take a revisionist position towards this School, which predominated in Germany at the beginning of the 20th century. In addition, sculptural and constructivist elements of a theatrical nature were added to Frankrühliah; they were lively and humorously personified[fig.5] and were inspired by three-dimensional works created by Oded. In the first stage, in an effort to distance himself from the innovations of Raphael Frank, Ezer reintroduced slanted lines, but very thin, and generated tension between them and their base and the upper horizontal stroke. In this way, perhaps not in a conscious manner, a dialogue was created between Oded and Didot, which brought the tension in form to an extreme level.

Throughout the stages of the work, the tone of the body of the letters is light, amusing and fearless, while at the same time respectful of their origin. While Frank relinquished the slanted upper horizontal stroke of the letter, Ezer decided to return the inclination of the letter only in the letter zain[fig.6], even if only in the name of giving pleasure and variety of form to the whole series. The letter final nun gets a lower base which did not exist originally but appears in several attempts to create Hebrew letters in the Art Nouveau style (as in Zev Raban and others). The colon and the semi-colon[fig.7] are full circles accompanied by strokes that are clearly characterized by the Jugendstil style, rather than being an original quotation.

Frankrühliah is a fascinating project thanks to the fine combination of searching experimentation without a clear objective, meticulousness in following rules to a certain extent, and the effort to preserve the serial nature of different signs in succession, like in commercial fonts. Although this was not the initial intention, Frankrühliah is being utilized for commercial needs, as a font like any other. At the same time, certain parts in the letter

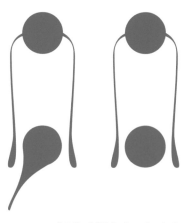

fig 8: ‘Frankrühliah' letters shin, tsadik and lamed

fig 9: ‘Frankrühliah' letter pey

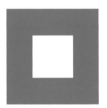

fig 10: ‘Haim' letter final mem

fig 11 a-c: Free style Letter designs from the first half of the 20th century

allow more space for personal expression. To borrow terms from the world of choreography, it is possible to say that, as in a ballet troupe, there are a number of prima ballerinas: the letters shin, final tsadik and lamed (fig.8) are impressive examples of additions and changes that perpetuate creativity in their design. In several instances, unusual design decisions in a standard font are noted. The letter samekh was rotated 180 degrees and is now on its upper horizontal line; also in the letter tsadik the hierarchies between its slants were changed, while the letter peh (fig.9) completely lost its base. Frankrühliah is a melody, a free and personal musical variation to the original from which it derives. It has a fresh visual approach, a love of the form, a deep appreciation for the spiritual father of the modern letter as well as a longing for the softness and romanticism that the Jugendstil School expressed so well as a reflection of its period. Thus, Raphael Frank and Oded Ezer finalize a cycle of 100 years of research on the borders of the Hebrew letter in a significant and fruitful dialogue.

Yan LeWit, a different kind of revolutionary, advertised the first version of the font Haim at the end of the 20's. Even an eye unfamiliar with the Hebrew language will easily distinguish the form of revolution that this font brought about. This was the first time that a Hebrew font appeared without serif, deliberately and with an awareness of the consequences. The act of omitting the serif is not merely a technical act or a choice not to rely on a calligraphic instrument. This act symbolizes the process of disengagement from the Jewish tradition, which a great number of Jewish people underwent parallel to the strengthening of the secular national identity. The creation of a secular Jewish centre in Israel and the influences of the modernist approach that were common in the Bauhaus in those times, provided the climate for the unambiguous statement that the Haim font brought with it. Yan LeWit indeed searched for a simple and geometric Hebrew letter form to function in parallel to Latin characters such as Futura, which were designed in the same years. However, he carved for himself a place of honour in the first row of typographic revolutionaries who pushed a slow evolutionary development in an unexpected and inconceivable direction in the eyes of many circles.

Not only did LeWit give up the serif, but he also increased the squareness of the letter, based on precise geometric structures, created 45 and 90 degree angles, squared the endings of the lines, and moreover, completely united the thickness of the vertical and horizontal strokes in the letter. In this way, he brought the Hebrew letter's form closest to its function as an abstract universal letter, devoid of national footprints leaning on place and religion. The final letter mem (fig.10) represented, in this font, more than any other, the greatest abstraction. It is, in fact, a whole square without any signs of a beginning or end in the act of writing.

In addition to font designers who devoted much attention and time to work whose declared objective was the design of new Hebrew fonts, anonymous artists too were experimenting with the form of letters. These experiments were not made for their own sake, but rather for practical purposes. Thanks to typographic aesthetics that came into being, these anonymous creators also entered the pantheon of Modern Hebrew typography. In the first half of the 20th century there were several instances of letter design in a free style, characterized by creative freedom (fig.11), unintentional humour, and a fascinating ability to improvise. These phenomena appeared mostly grounded in the practical need.

The orthodox communities, for instance, needed to transfer information in Hebrew within their communities. To this end, letters were specially designed to meet such needs as: seals of various types, posters, print objects and commercial signs. In non-religious sectors, new formats appeared such as local newspaper headlines, Independence Day posters, street signs, bank names, advertising billboards, packages, book covers and other graphic products. In all these instances, creativity and innovation in letter design were a requirement to fulfil the visual niche created by the rapid awakening of the Hebrew language. Local typographical design of this kind was lively, yielding a wealth of forms and innovativeness in the field of letter form. This reality was "hungry" for fresh, innovative ideas in letter form, it was missing them, and constituted a catalyst for their creation. Letter designers were painters, sign designers, carvers, sculptors, draftsmen, carpenters and builders whose anonymous work flourished in those years. HaGilda, a gild established in 2002 as a cooperative by Oded Ezer, Michal Sahar and Danny Meirav (its leader) responded to these anonymous creators. The love of fonts, the awareness of a scarcity of Hebrew fonts and the desire to experiment with the process of font design brought them together. A number of the fonts designed by HaGilda was a resuscitation and preservation of the same letters used in the first decades of the 20th century (fig.12). Members of HaGilda related to this work as a unique national mission. In parallel to the work of remodelling, the members of the guild developed new fonts taking into account contemporary ergonomic and commercial components. There is no doubt that the difference between the approaches of the non-committed veteran letter artists on one hand, and the practical commercial designers' approach on the other, clearly defined for Oded the character of the path he had already tread for several years.

The Hadassah font, published in 1958, was designed by Henri Friedlaender. While designing the letter, he too, like his predecessors, was unaware of the extent of innovation to be contained in the letter in its final form. It seems that the design and the preliminary research in ancient Hebrew manuscripts are testimony to the desire to preserve and continue an evolutionary sequence that existed already. Nonetheless, Friedlaender aspired to succeed at creating new forms that would not be dependent exclusively on past heritage. Unlike contemporary font designers such as Yanek Yontef, Michal Sahar, Oded Ezer, and others, the social, political, technological background and circumstances eventually influenced the characteristics of Friedlaender's revolution.

The shape of the serif in the Hadassah letters (fig.13) testifies to the desire to make a break from forms derived from calligraphic writing. The serif in Hadassah is dominant and inclined to the left – which increases movement in the entire letter, giving rise to a square and drawn serif not present at the outset of writing . This is a common phenomenon in traditional Hebrew writings made with a quill pen or plume. In addition, the clear and strong characteristic of the diagonal lines without ornaments was salient. The meeting points between the upper horizontal lines of the letters and the diagonal lines are softly designed, strong and optically prominent. Here, too, the drawing hand is visible, rather than the calligraphic one. Since then, Hadassah has been considered a unique, exceptional and breakthrough font, with a strong, independent personality.

An additional example of a work process derived from a classical ergonomic need, that nevertheless yielded revolutionary products, are the letter fonts Oron, published in the mid 60's in Israel. Asher Oron, the font designer, may be included in the group of pragmatic font designers. For this group of designers, the functionality of the letter, the definition of its objectives, as well as a "correctness" of its structure are significant components in the form development of the letter. However, 50 years after its publication, it is possible to say that Oron is almost an underground font in comparison to the preservation of the Jewish character of the Hebrew letter and its continuity with its predecessors. The most prominent distinction in this font is the revolution undergone in the thickness of the strokes. Here, for the first time, the diagonal strokes in the letter became the prominent strong lines whereas the horizontal strokes became relatively thin, which was totally foreign to the classical form of the Hebrew letter. Indeed, this decision was made in view of the definition of the font as the Hebrew parallel to the Latin Universal, although the meaning that emerges from this decision is revolutionary. More specific issues too symbolize the resulting revolution: the form of the connection of the upper horizontal strokes of the letter bet to its base, the upper horizontal strokes of the letters vav, yod, lamed, mem, final nun (fig.14), the connection between the two strokes of the letter final tsadik, and especially, the detachment of the middle stroke of the letter shin from its base. These are all innovations in the form of the Hebrew letters in relation to what existed until the emergence of the font.

Reminiscences of a form characteristics of Oron are visible in the font Erika as well, designed in 1992, and in the font Foodi, designed in 2004, both by the typographer and font designer Yanek Yontef. These fonts were designed, similarly to Oron, out of a need for a purely practical, commercial font, but embody the hues of Oron's revolution: the

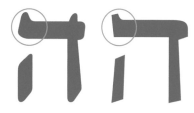

fig 12: Ha'Gilda exhibition poster and fonts catalog

fig 13: 'Hadassah' vs. 'Shoken' serifs

fig 14: Upper strokes of 'Oron'

upper horizontal strokes of the letters bet, heh, khet, resh, taf, become rounded, a phenomenon considered as new in the styling of the Hebrew letters. The letter peh becomes more rounded than in Oron and becomes more oval in shape. In the letter tsadik, there is a break in its diagonal central axis. This break appears only once in this font, and looks exceptionally groundbreaking in its innovativeness. This case illustrates that sometimes a single letter in a font may constitute a source of inspiration for future font designers.

This is true also of Oded Ezer, who is by nature curious and adventurous like a child, editing his typographic experiments out of a deep consciousness of the sequence of which he is a part. He works out of an awareness of the early evolution of the Hebrew letter and of the 20th century. Oded also realizes the influences that his experimental work may exert on those who will follow him, as well as the resistance they may provoke. In recent years, his work fluctuates between the experimental and the commercial, with a constant willingness to monitor the quality of dialogue between them. In the framework of his research work, he usually mixes the materials of both extremes. He draws inspiration, joy and strength from his predecessors, who did not play down their typographic experiments and did not recoil from criticism and rejection of their work. As we have learned from the past, works that were ahead of their time need an extra period of time in order to become accepted. It seems that we are approaching this time.

COMPOUNDS AND MIXTURES

Oded Ezer's work is exceptional in the landscape of local work in Israel. It attracts attention both for the fresh typographic products it yields and, moreover, for its character and meaning today and influence in the future. Leafing through his font catalogue, and viewing his works on site, immediately provoke a strong feeling for the materials with which he works, a joy of living and the mischievous connotation of a boy who at any moment might do something to embarrass the adults around him because he is endangering a sacred truth. A brief inspection of example pages from the specimen catalogue shows the broad spectrum in which Ezer works. This space ranges between the practical and precise, the non-committed, the amusing, a lack of rules and borders.

Oded Ezer testifies that he moves between the two extremes, enjoying both, at times confusing the two and realizing that it is something in their combination to which he aspires. The uncomfortable movement between these two extremes of the spectrum is intensified beyond the personal. As a designer living and working in Israel, he is also aware of the responsibility entailed in his work and understands that he is a party to the cultural dilemma in which creators in parallel disciplines find themselves. To what extent are we grounded in a cultural soil? How much freedom can we take without becoming detached so our works lose touch with the local historical and social context? Any experiment that takes place in Oded's typographic laboratory assumes the danger that the products of the experiment will not be perceived as typography or even as Hebrew.

What is the stage at which the line turns from a display of the DNA of a letter into a pointless line? How is it possible to work simultaneously with abstract forms and relate to them as letters as well? Are the answers to these questions entirely subjective? This dual condition, of the yearning for experimentation and self-expression vis-à-vis the need to present commercial products that enjoy wide acceptance and understanding, generates discomfort and confusion. This duality is expressed also in the conflict between the personal language and the "national responsibility" concerning the design of new forms. Therefore it seems at times that the catalogue and the posters were made in two different places, by two different creators.

In the year 2006, Oded published the Bet Hillel font [fig.15]. The specimen page of the font projects eloquence and professionalism. The page presents the two scales of the font and patches of text in small print, the way most fonts are displayed when for sale. The story behind the decision of the font design, the work process and the final result indicate the complexity of Ezer's creation. The project started from a tribute to the Hazvi font designer – Zvi Housmann, who designed this font during the 1950's. Over the years, this font came to be perceived as obsolete and its use decreased. Furthermore, the typographic qualities and the innovativeness in the font stimulated Oded to start his work. His starting point was similar to that at the time of the guild. During his work, the intention was that the font be used mainly as a title font to be supplemented with new signs that did not exist in the Hazvi font. The design work was intuitive and based simultaneously on form and contents in the Hebrew language and its preservation. During the work, some changes occurred in the width of the vertical lines and they became thin in comparison to the original font (fig.16). Consequently, a new dominant characteristic was created in Bet Hillel which is the special connection between the upper horizontal and the vertical strokes of the letters. As the font design approached completion, it became clear that the font could also be used as a text font. Moreover, when focusing on the parts in a single letter, it is possible to identify far-fetched decisions characteristic of a typographer–experimental artist. The design of the serif as seen in the letter ain (fig.17), for instance, is a brave act, which can apparently take the font to a non-practical place, surely not the use in long texts. The deformations and the sharp transitions between the parts of the letter seem like a puzzling promise of a new form. However, the font succeeds at meeting the professional requirements of an all-purpose font and the creative needs and freedom of expression of thoughts simultaneously. The final product is fascinating; although distant from the Hazvi, it proves that it is possible to successfully embody two positions in the same font: experimental and classical.

The project might not have reached its position if the process had not been supported by an imaginary story devised by Oded. In the story, he goes back in time to the years when the Hazvi font was designed, meets with Zvi Housmann and together they mull over the issue of the form of Bet Hillel. The final product is actually the fruit of the conjoined work of two people: is it relevant that one of them passed away a long time ago?

The Ezer Classic project, still in stages of creation, signals the beginning of a new era in Oded Ezer's work. In this project, the ambition to design a useful font based on calligraphic foundations meets the desire to involve creativity and creation of new personal fragments. In the first stage, Oded sketched the "skeletons" or the DNA of the classical Hebrew letters in a Sephardic, Jerusalemite, as well as the relatively new Ezer Block font. The new stage was pure calligraphy. Oded, assisted by Mr. Nisgav, drew the prototype of the Hebrew letters based on these axes, with the help of a quill pen. This was the basis for the continuation of the work. It is important to point out that the Ezer Classic project is the most complex to date produced by Oded purposefully in work stages and collaboratively with others. Subsequent to the examination of several pages on which form experiments were made with some letters, the calligraphic formulae versions were selected as the basis for the continuation of the work. At this stage, Ezer made an abstraction of the calligraphic letters and a break took place from the exclusive commitment to the writing tool. This is the most fascinating stage in the work, in its permeable transition from discipline and regularity to the abstract and experimental. Here the first encounter between the two extremes occurred, which had not occurred until that moment in Ezer's work. However, even after the process of abstraction, some optical problems remained in the font, especially while reading the text. To this end, Oded approached Frankrühlia, where optical and form solutions were learned, and implemented them in the advanced raw materials of Ezer Classic.

The final product of this font projects maturity, ripeness, and is the fruit of important conclusions reached by Oded Ezer. In this project, he proves to himself that there is a way to internalize and inculcate the logic and conclusions from existing texts and integrate them in a contemporary work that is not satisfied with merely renovating and resuscitating. Ezer Classic is a compound and not a mixture, to borrow terms from the laboratory. A reaction ensued, connecting between all the components, forming a legible product based on clear logic and regularity, while fresh, innovating and surprising at the same time. Apparently, one wonders whether the process of work and the result are different in Ezer's work compared to that of Zvi Narkiss in the design of the Narkiss Linotype font

Beit-Hilel_OE Light

Beit-Hilel_OE Heavy

fig 15: **'Beit Hillel' by Oded Ezer**

fig 16: **Letter gimel of 'Hatzvi' vs. 'Beit Hillel'**

fig 17: **Letter ein of 'Hatzvi' vs. 'Beit Hillel'**

fig 14: **Upper strokes of 'Oron'**

dated from the beginning of the 50's. The beauty in the distinction between the two is in their handwritings. Zvi Narkiss remained loyal to the calligraphic tradition. The additions he created in the font are light and perceived as minor corrections. Oded Ezer tries in the Ezer Classic Project to perpetuate the calligraphic presence while at the same time allowing himself wider self-expression than Narkiss without damaging the quality of the letter itself.

THE BIOCHEMISTRY OF THE LETTER

A number of questions concerning Oded Ezer's multi-faceted work arise from an interim summary: What is the nature of the dialogue between the pragmatic and the experimental? Is the work of font design destined to remain restrained to the point of anonymity of the creator's handwriting? Is the experimental responsible for creating the coming future, opening channels and discovering new territories? Is the character of these two lines of work opposed and impossible to connect? Where, if at all, is the uncommitted borderline between the collective, the communicative and the personal?

The development process emerging in Oded Ezer's work testifies to the ability to rely simultaneously on a number of starting points in a mature, quiet and wide ranging place. The virtuosity of preserving the child, curious and adventurous, who does not depend on anyone or anything other than the experience of discovery, as well as experience and professional maturity are unique and important. Whereas in the past experimentalism was considered as less relevant in the typical areas of font design, today the field is receiving more and more recognition and does not lose in importance to theoretical research dealing with morphological change in the Hebrew letter.

fig 18: 'Futura' letters by Paul Renner

Paul Renner came from similar starting points at the time he drafted his first sketches of Futura in 1924 (fig.18). From these early sketches it is possible to get the impression of a preoccupation with forms without footprints or constraints. A number of versions which are not in use at all were added to some letters but they ask existential questions regarding what is considered as a and when it becomes an addend without any concrete meaning. The letter g, for instance, was created solely from basic forms, circle, rectangle, triangle, similarly to the modernistic approach that was consolidated at the same time in the Bauhaus. In the same years, Herbert Beyer designed the Universal, based on basic lines in clear geometric forms. The Futura font fulfils all the strict parameters of a text and title font, and is widely used to this day in a variety of graphic works.

It is possible that it is still too soon to define or identify, but Oded Ezer signals the beginning of a trend that will expand. This trend is characterized by a wide approach in the area of font design, while using raw materials from different and opposing worlds and with a flexibility that enables the spontaneous transition from a minute ruler. If we try to imagine a return in time so that Oded can meet anonymous creators from the 20's and the 30's, we will find a similar common joy and freedom of work. The difference will obviously be in the level of awareness of the context in which the work takes place and an innocence which was replaced by responsibility.

Yehuda Hofshi graduated from the Bezalel Academy of Arts and Design in Jerusalem. He divides his time between research writing in Hebrew typography issues, lecturing in academic institutions and working as designer in the studio he directs.

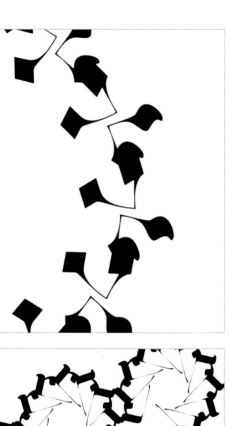
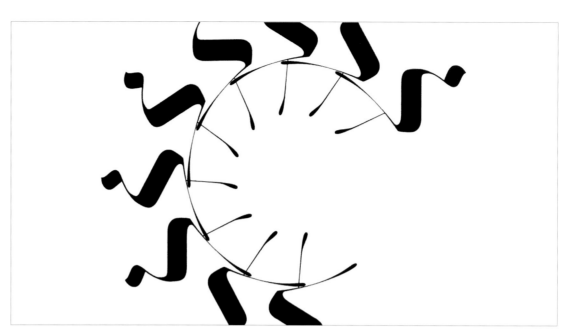

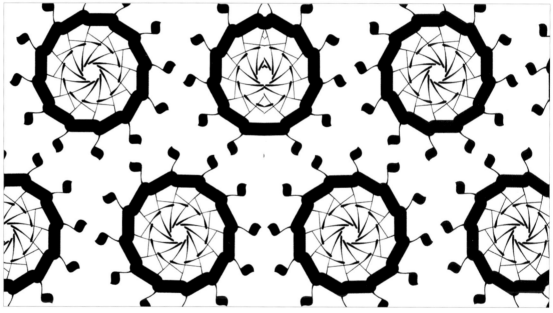
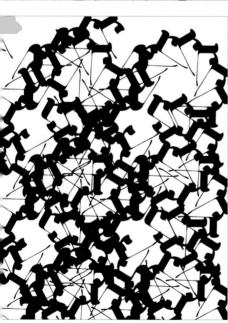

Fonts Oded Ezer

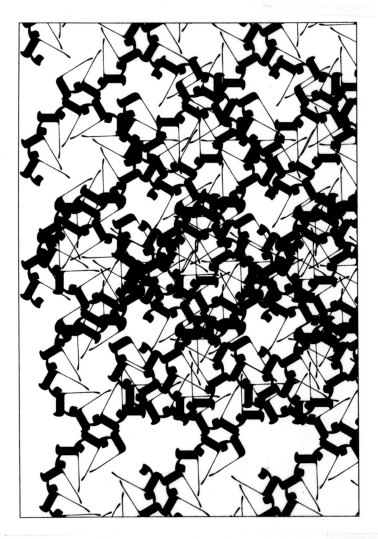

Notebooks
Designed in cooperation with Anat Safra

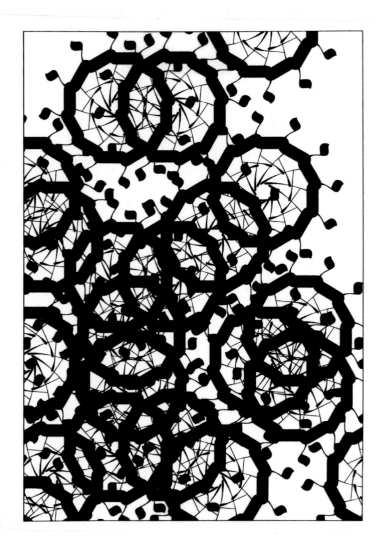

Patterns made of Frankrühliah letters
2008

פתיחת התערוכה בשבת 11.9.04 בשעה 11:00 | אוצרים: מורין רוזן ומשה פנחסי

אגודת הציירים והפסלים בישראל, חיפה והצפון (ע.ר.)
בית האמנים ע"ש שאגאל, שד' הציונות 24, חיפה. טל.8522355
The Israel Painters & Sculptors Association (R.A.)
Haifa & Northern District Chagall House, 24 Zionut Ave. Tel. 8522355

משרד החינוך התרבות והספורט
מנהל התרבות, המחלקה למוזיאונים ואומנות פלסטית

בבית אגודת הציירים, חיפה, שד' הציונות 24 | בין התאריכים 8.9.04-27.9.04

הגלריה פתוחה בימים א'-ה' 09:00-13:00, 16:00-19:00, שבת 10:00-13:00

-6399732 :עיצוב

Invitation for an exhibition using Frankrühliah and Alchemist typefaces
2004

Page for Spatium Magazine featuring two "typography" logos using Frankrühliah and Maya letters
2004

Frankrühliah (by Oded Ezer, 2003) vs. Frank
Rühl (Raphael Frank, 1908)

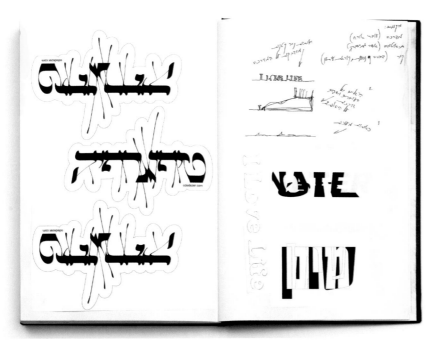

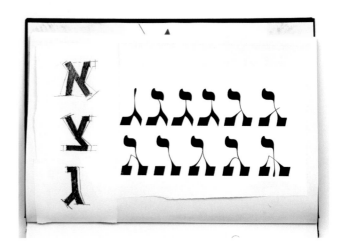

Sketches of Frankrühliah typeface
2001 - 2003

0123456789

Tipografya poster
Self-produced, 2004
B/W process printing, 68 x 94 cm

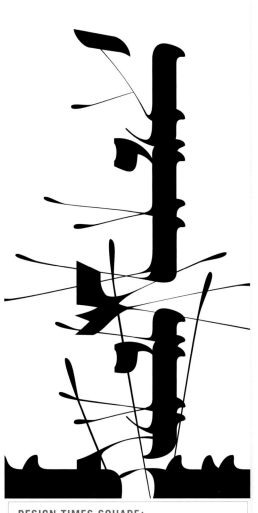

DESIGN TIMES SQUARE:
THE URBAN FOREST PROJECT
ODED EZER

TIMES
SQUARE
ALLIANCE

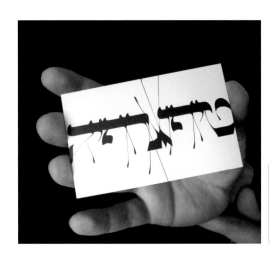

Typographic tree
for the Urban Forest Project, 2006

Tipografya logo
on a business card, 2006

Oded wearing the T(ypography)-shirt!
2006

The T(ypography)-shirt!
won second prize at the second T-1 International
T-shirt design competition, Tokyo, 2006

(Following pages) **Calligraphic studies for Ezer**
Classic typeface
2007-2008

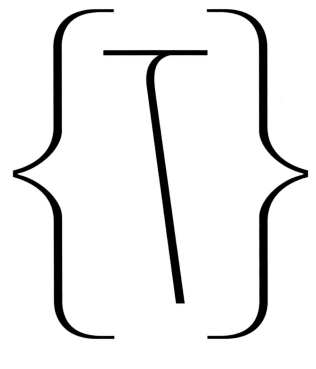

אלכימאי דקיק

אבגדהוזחטיכלמנסעפ
צקרשת רםוףץ456789
;",.:שם$ # = + ?!*>]{)(0123
({[<%‾–/.'

אלכימאי דקיק נטוי

אבגדהוזחטיכלמנסעפ
צקרשת רםוףץ456789
;",.:שם$ # = + ?!*>]{)(0123
({[<%‾–/.'

אלכימאי דקיק

Specimen for Alchemist typeface
1999 – 2004

Specimen for Frankrühliah typeface
2001 – 2003

אבגדהוז

אבגדהוז

אבגדהו

אבגדהו

אבגדה

אבגדה

תאגיד קליל
Taagid_OE UltraLight
אבגדהוזחטיכלמנסעפצקרשתרםוףץ
({[<*;:?!'""$₪/=+#%) 1234567890

תאגיד קל
Taagid_OE Light
אבגדהוזחטיכלמנסעפצקרשתרםוףץ
({[<*;:?!'""$₪/=+#%) 1234567890

תאגיד רגיל
Taagid_OE Regular
אבגדהוזחטיכלמנסעפצקרשתרםוףץ
({[<*;:?!'""$₪/=+#%) 1234567890

תאגיד שמן
Taagid_OE Bold
אבגדהוזחטיכלמנסעפצקרשתרםוףץ
({[<*;:?!'""$₪/=+#%) 1234567890

תאגיד שחור
Taagid_OE Black
אבגדהוזחטיכלמנסעפצקרשתרםוףץ
({[<*;:?!'""$₪/=+#%) 1234567890

תאגיד אולטרא
Taagid_OE Ultra
אבגדהוזחטיכלמנסעפצקרשתרםוףץ
({[<*;:?!'""$₪/=+#%) 1234567890

דוגמת טקסט: תאגיד רגיל

שקדם להקמת המדינה, ליו
מראשית דרכה. מדינת ישר
במיוחד את המשחק העממי
ציוני כאשר היה לה צורך ב
אפוף אפוא בסממני הלאום
מפה היסטורית ראשונית וח

דוגמת טקסט: תאגיד קל

שקדם להקמת המדינה, ליווה
מראשית דרכה. מדינת ישראל
את המשחק העממי הזה, ידעו
היה לה צורך בכך, והכדורגל ה
בסממני הלאומיות הציונית־יה
ראשונית וחלוצית של הכדורג׳

Specimen for Ta'agid typeface
2006

Sketches for the logo of Bank Hapoalim

that where later on developed into the Alchemist
typeface, 2000

**Specimens for different
Hebrew typefaces**
1998 - 2008

נוה־צדק קל   NeveZedek_OE Light
אבגדהוזחטיכלמנסעפצקרשתרסוףץ
({[<*;:?!'"$₪/=+#%) 1234567890

נוה־צדק שמן   NeveZedek_OE Bold
אבגדהוזחטיכלמנסעפצקרשתרסוףץ
({[<*;:?!'"$₪/=+#%) 1234567890

שלוותה קל   Shalvata_OE Light
אבגדהוזחטיכלמנסעפצקרשתרסוףץ
({[<*;:?!'"$₪/=+#%) 1234567890

שלוותה כבד   Shalvata_OE Heavy
אבגדהוזחטיכלמנסעפצקרשתרסוףץ
({[<*;:?!'"$₪/=+#%) 1234567890

אנמיה   Anemia_OE
אבגדהוזחטיכלמנסעפצקרשתר
({[;:?!$₪/=+#%1234567890

אנמיה אלט   Anemia_OE Alt
אבגדהוזחטיכלמנסעפצקרשתך
({[;:?!$₪/=+#%1234567890

סוסיתא קל   Susita_OE Light
אבגדהוזחטיכלמנסעפצקרשתרסוףץ
({[<*;:?!'"$₪/=+#%) 1234567890

סוסיתא כבד   Susita_OE Heavy
אבגדהוזחטיכלמנסעפצקרשתרסוףץ
({[<*;:?!'"$₪/=+#%) 1234567890

בית־הלל קל   Beit-Hilel_OE Light
אבגדהוזחטיכלמנסעפצקרשתרסוףץ
({[<*;:?!'"$₪/=+#%) 1234567890

בית־הלל כבד   Beit-Hilel_OE Heavy
אבגדהוזחטיכלמנסעפצקרשתרסוףץ
({[<*;:?!'"$₪/=+#%) 1234567890

תאגיד קליל   Taagid_OE UltraLight
אבגדהוזחטיכלמנסעפצקרשתרסוףץ
({[<*;:?!'"$₪/=+#%) 1234567890

תאגיד אולטרא   Taagid_OE Ultra
אבגדהוזחטיכלמנסעפצקרשתרסוףץ
({[<*;:?!'"$₪/=+#%) 1234567890

מעודד־פשוט רגיל   MeodedPashut_OE Regular
אבגדהוזחטיכלמנסעפצקרשתרסוףץ
({[<*;:?!'"$₪/=+#%) 1234567890

מעודד־פשוט שחור   MeodedPashut_OE Black
אבגדהוזחטיכלמנסעפצקרשתרסוףץ
({[<*;:?!'"$₪/=+#%) 1234567890

סיסטזה קל   Systeza_OE Light
אבגדהוזחטיכלמנסעפצקרשתרסוףץ
({[<*;:?!'"$₪/=+#%) 1234567890

סיסטזה טרנדי   Systeza_OE Trendy
אבגדהוזחטיכלמנסעפצקרשתרסוףץ
({[<*;:?!'"$₪/=+#%) 1234567890

Ezer's Classic typeface
still in progress

35

סיסטזה קל Systeza_OE Light
אבגדהוזחטיכלמנסעפצקרשתרסוףץ
(}{][<*;:?!''"$₪/=+#%) 1234567890

סיסטזה רגיל Systeza_OE Regular
אבגדהוזחטיכלמנסעפצקרשתרסוףץ
(}{][<*;:?!''"$₪/=+#%) 1234567890

סיסטזה שמן Systeza_OE Light
אבגדהוזחטיכלמנסעפצקרשתרסוףץ
(}{][<*;:?!''"$₪/=+#%) 1234567890

סיסטזה כבד Systeza_OE Heavy
אבגדהוזחטיכלמנסעפצקרשתרסוףץ
(}{][<*;:?!''"$₪/=+#%) 1234567890

דוגמת טקסט: סיסטזה קל טו פ'
שקדם להקמת המדינה, ליווה אותה בצייתנות ובהכנעה
מראשית דרכה. מדינת ישראל, שמנהיגיה לא העריכו במיוחד
את המשחק העממי הזה, ידעה לעשות בו שימוש ציוני כאשר

דוגמת טקסט: סיסטזה רגיל טו פ'
שקדם להקמת המדינה, ליווה אותה בצייתנות ובהכנעה
מראשית דרכה. מדינת ישראל, שמנהיגיה לא העריכו במיוחד
את המשחק העממי הזה, ידעה לעשות בו שימוש ציוני

סיסטזה טרנדי Systeza_OE Trendy
אבגדהוזחטיכלמנסעפצקרשתרסוףץ
(}{][<*;:?!''"$₪/=+#%) 1234567890

אימפקטה קל Impacta_OE Light
אבגדהוזחטיכלמנסעפצקרשתרסוףץ
[][<*;:?!''"$₪/=+#%] 1234567890

אימפקטה Impacta_OE
אבגדהוזחטיכלמנסעפצקרשתרסוףץ
[][<*;:?!''"$₪/=+#%] 1234567890

אימפקטה קל נטוי Impacta_OE LightItalic
אבגדהוזחטיכלמנסעפצקרשתרסוףץ
[][<*;:?!''"$₪/=+#%] 1234567890

אימפקטה נטוי Impacta_OE Italic
אבגדהוזחטיכלמנסעפצקרשתרסוףץ
[][<*;:?!''"$₪/=+#%] 1234567890

נווה־צדק קל NeveZedek_OE Light
אבגדהוזחטיכלמנסעפצקרשתרסוףץ
(}{][<*;:?!''"$₪ /=+#%) 1234567890

נווה־צדק רגיל NeveZedek_OE Regular
אבגדהוזחטיכלמנסעפצקרשתרסוףץ
(}{][<*;:?!''"$₪ /=+#%) 1234567890

**Pages from Oded
Ezer's font catalog**

Fonts Oded Ezer

Font catalogue
2006

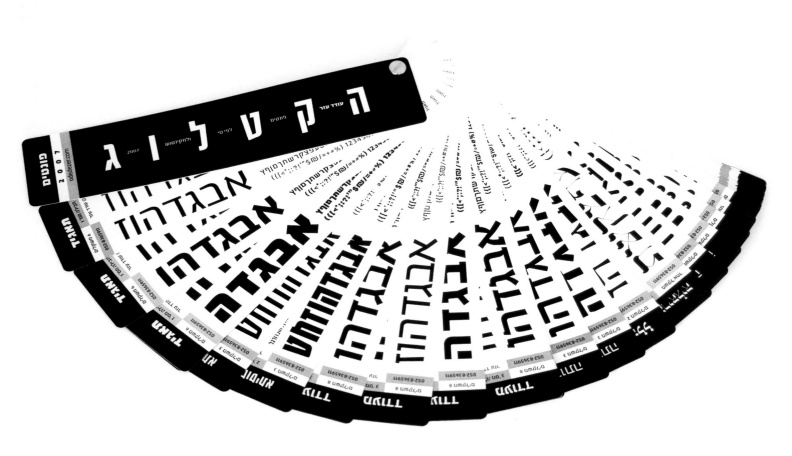

Font catalogue
2007

Pages from Ha'Gilda fonts catalog
2004
Ha'Gilda is the first Israeli cooperative of font
designers that was co-founded by Oded in 2002

Greeting cards for Noble Works Inc.
New York, using Latin version of
Frankrühliah typeface

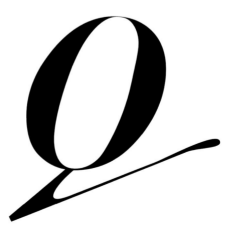

Anemia, mono-space font
Designed by Oded Ezer (2000)

Neve-Zedek, text font
Designed by Oded Ezer (2001)

Koren, serif text font
Designed by Eliyahu Koren (1958)

Hatzvi, sans-serif display font
Designed by Tzvi Hausmann (1956)

Eden, Display font
Designed by Oded Ezer (1998)

Miryam, sans-serif text & display font
Unknown designer (1918)

Maya, Sans-serif display font
Designed by Oded Ezer (1998)

Drogolin, a classic serif text font
Unknown designer (19th c.)

Hayim, sans-serif display font
Designed by Yaakov Hayim Levit (1933)

Alchemist Square, Sans-serif text & display font
Designed by Oded Ezer (2003)

Hadassah, serif text & display font
Designed by Henry Friedlander (1958)

Alchemist, Sans-serif text & display font
Designed by Oded Ezer (2000)

David serif text font
Designed by Itamar David (1952)

Kafka, display font
Designed by Oded Ezer (1999)

Aharoni, sans-serif display font
Designed by Tuvya Aharoni (1938)

Sars, display font
Designed by Oded Ezer (2003)

Frank-Rühl, a classic serif text font
Designed by Raphael Frank (1910)

Systeza, display font
Designed by Oded Ezer
Based on Fabrizio Schiavi

Shoken, serif text font
Designed by Franziska Baruch (1943)

Impacta, sans-serif display font
Designed by Oded Ezer (1999)

Rashi, traditional serif font
Unknown designer

Frankrihlya, 'ornamental' font
Designed by Oded Ezer (2002)

Double spread from Spatium magazine
with Oded's typefaces (left) and classic twentieth century
Hebrew typefaces (right), 2004

Oded Ezer with Zvi Narkiss
one of the establishers of modern Hebrew type design

Calligraphic studies

NPI "When I had just graduated from Bezalel Academy, I knew that I wanted to do something new and to surprise myself. I realized that in order to do something revolutionary, I needed time. I knew that only working for clients wouldn't make me happy because I would have to stick to their rules, but it was the only way to make money. So the name "non-profit item" came to my mind and I decided to call my nocturnal activities NPI. Since I am a graphic designer, after all, I needed a logo for that. In the beginning, I stamped every work I did at night with it. I really needed that in my early stage, because nobody had told me that this kind of work was a legitimate process. I needed to label it somehow. The design was inspired by the traditional chocolate and coffee manufacturer, 'Elite', that was based in my home town, Ramat Gan. If you were growing up in there in the 70's, you couldn't escape from the heavy chocolate smell that hovered like a cloud above the city. The Elite logo was designed in 1933 by Austrian-Jewish-Israeli graphic artist Franz Krausz, a pioneer in his field and one of the best masters that ever worked in my country. Although the original logo that Krausz designed had already been replaced and abandoned in the late 60's, it was still curved in stone on the facade of the famous building until 2007, when it was destroyed by a new landlord. For me, it became an icon representing sweetness, sunny afternoons and childhood nostalgia. When thinking about an appropriate personal logo for my experimental activities back in 2000, it was only natural for me to make a fun revival of this neglected symbol that, through a wonderful coincidence, carries a monogram of my own name - the Hebrew letter 'Ayin', for my first name - together with the Latin letter 'yE', for my last name."

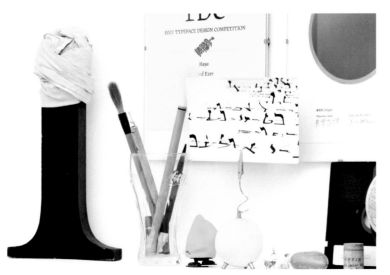

Graphic Work
Always play, never work

by <u>Kitty Bolhöfer</u>

IT REALLY IS A SHAME THAT ONE MUST LEAF THROUGH THE PAGES OF CHILDREN'S BOOKS TO BE TRULY AMAZED BY POP-UPS – TWISTING AND TURNING, FOLDING, SWELLING, JUMPING UP TO CREATE INCREDIBLE BUILDINGS.

∞ Letter-like creatures, striking installations made of pink chewing gum or nails, letters that conquer the human body – a sort of haptic poetry on the border of legibility – has become Oded Ezer's trademark. However, as a successful typographer, his work consists not only of establishing his own design; it also means creating trademarks for clients, a discipline that implies specifications, restrictions and compromises. His commercial work seems so far removed from the imaginative, sometimes dadaistic installations and posters of the playroom, that one can only wonder how he bridges this gap without being torn apart. Well, if it is true that genius and madness are closely related, then the mastermind's reaction to this tricky situation is quite logical: Oded splits his personality and develops two almost antithetical personas, each of which grows stronger as it leaves a mark on its particular field. This modus operandi is anything but a makeshift arrangement; from time to time he interconnects these two like brain hemispheres, exchanging the obtained knowledge and thus completing the mind of the overall artist.

When it comes to corporate assignments, whether this means creating logos, covers for CDs and books or layouts for magazines and newspapers, the graphic designer inside Oded attends to the work. His way of working is primarily characterized by dedication to his clients because, as a contractor, he highly respects the confidence they have in him. Thus, he structures the process in a timetable beforehand and thoroughly researches everything there is to learn about the project such as the nature of the business, the company or the product, its essence, personality and exact values, the audience or users and the competitor's visual language. The results are precisely recorded in a brief that serves as a basis for the project. When the rational part of the preparatory work is completed, the typo artist Oded drops in. Sometimes he even brings findings from his experimental journeys and, in a joint venture, the two indulge in long sketching sessions that adhere to only one rule: always play, never work. By hand or on the computer, they draft between ten and thirty sketches which Oded, the graphic designer, then narrows down to a small selection for the client. Through his work experience, he knows exactly what a good logo requires: it has to be easily remembered, it needs to be iconic in nature and it should become part of people's lives and memories. With cultural depth on one hand and surprising simplicity on the other, it has to remain 'fresh' even a hundred years after its creation. Above all, a good logo has to serve the people's needs more than those of the client or designer. However, it takes a great deal of communication and several rounds of this procedure to achieve the desired result.

The two personas within Oded Ezer both find passion and satisfaction within their strikingly different fields; and as incongruous as they may be, they are inseparable. Furthermore, they feed each other with expertise and balance each other out. Thus, the graphic designer and the typo artist together enable the overall person Oded to cover this vast range of works, reducing the gap between what he feels graphic design should be and what the market demands. By creating two, sometimes even more alter egos, he can now appreciate commercial work more than at the outset, but also, by standing his ground as an experimental typographer over the years, the market has finally recognized this potential and is now approaching Oded – and that is sheer madness.

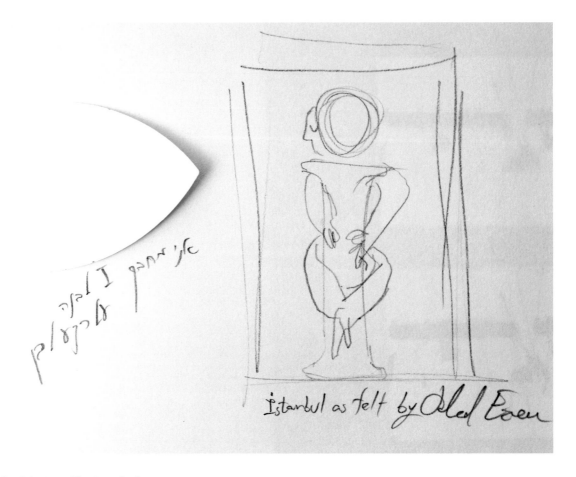

Sketches and final design of 'I ♥ Istanbul'
poster for Grafist exhibition
Istanbul, 2007

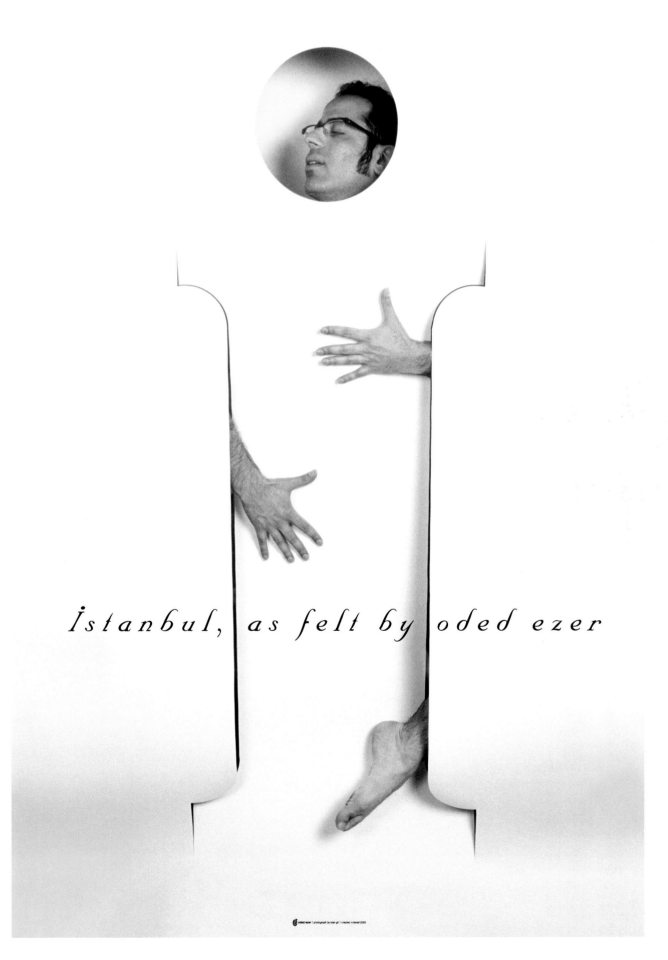

İstanbul, as felt by oded ezer

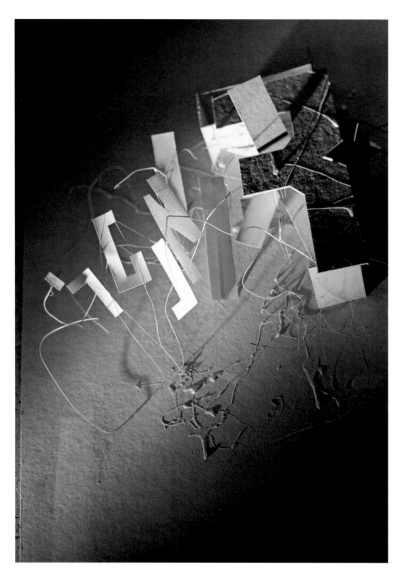

**Model, poster and booklet for the
Israel Forum for Co-Productions**
2000

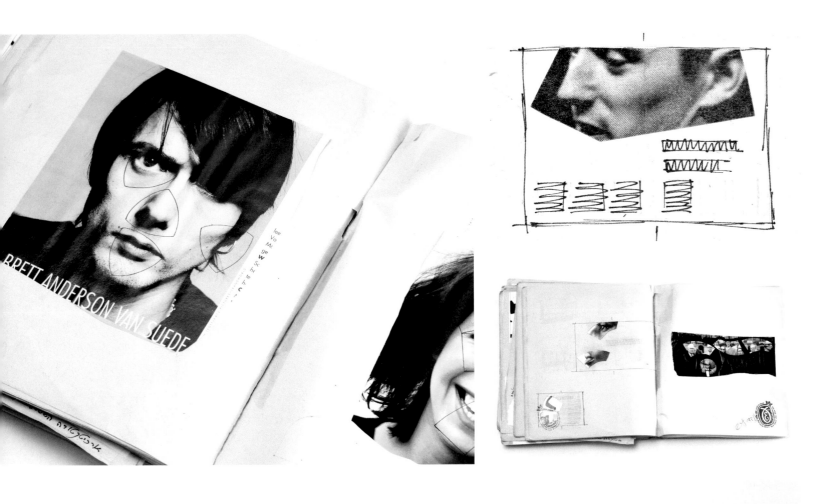

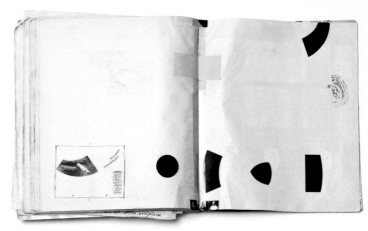

ezer!shapes "The initial shapes for the poster originate from a furniture catalogue I found on the street in Amsterdam. Those are shapes of tabletops that one could take out and lay on floor plans in order to design the interior of one's apartment. I liked these strange shapes and immediately wanted to do something with them, so I used them as a basis for a dingbat font that resulted in a poster. I used the outline of the shapes as a background for a single shape in the foreground. I did it only because it looked very beau-tiful to me. This work made me think about structures in an architectural way and later led to posters like 'The Chorus of the Opera' or 'Co-Pro2000'. This was one of the only posters I did on the computer. Later on, I avoided the computer as a working tool because I feel that it was limiting me. In my experimental work, I now use it only as a production or retouching tool."

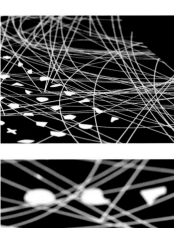

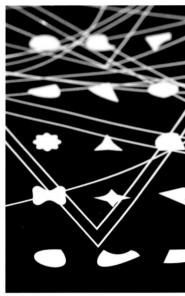

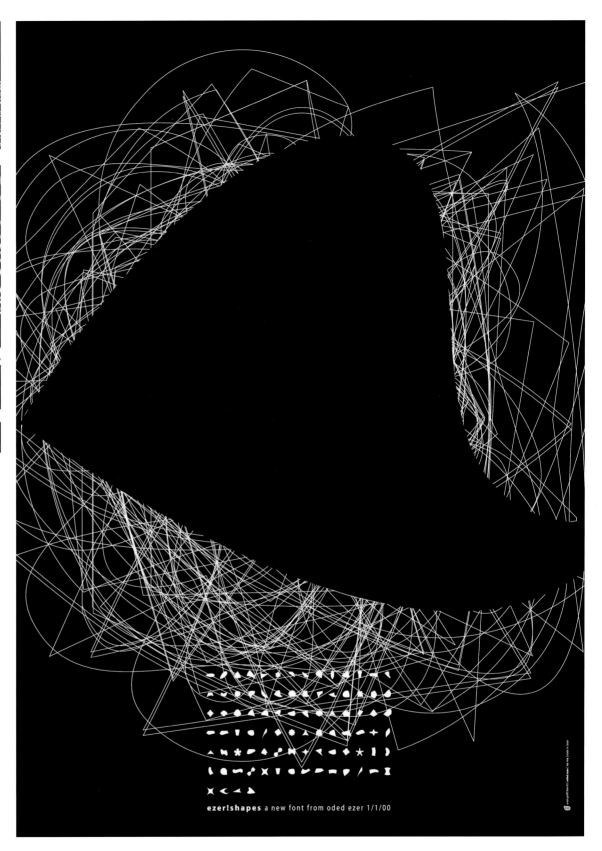

ezer!shapes a new font from oded ezer 1/1/00

<u>Graphic Work</u> Oded Ezer

Ha'Gilda exhibition poster
2005

Font catalogue cover and logo
designed in cooperation with Michal Sahar, 2004

עודד עזר גאה להציג אות עברית חדשה:

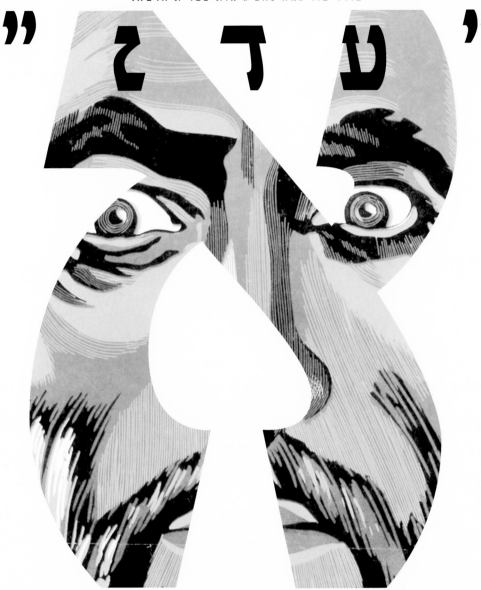

"עדן"

אבגדההווזחטיכ‬כלמנסםעפףצץקרשתםרסזףץוס‪‫0123456789 ‭(}{"$'%‮שׁ‬*+,.־/.;:=;?!)

אבגדההווזחטיכ‬כלמנסםעפעףצץקרשתםרסזףץוס‪‫0123456789 ‭(}{"$'%‮שׁ‬*+,.־/.;:=;?!)

 אות הכותרת "עדן כבד" נוצרה בהשראה אותיות מצוירות ביד על גבי כרזות קולנוע שפרסמה בתי הקולנוע התל־אביבי "עדן" ו"אופיר" במהלך שנות השלושים. שמות הכוכבים הראשיים צוירו על פי רוב ביד ציורי אותיות אלה נסרקו, ונחברו הבדלי הסמגנונת הרדים בניהם. לאחר מכן נתחחו סרי האופי העיקריים של אותיות אלה על מנת שישמשו בסים לעיצוב פונט דיגיטלי מחוחשב. בשלב הבא העברה הנתונים לתכנה מתאימה ונוצבה האות. הציוב המחודש הוסף אות זו לפעילה וניתן להשתמש כה כמחשב מסינטוש.

אות הכותרת "עדן כבד" נוצרה בהשראה אותיות מצוירות ביד על גבי כרזות קולנוע שפרסם בית הקולנוע התל־אביבי "עדן" במהלך שנות השלושים. לגבי רוב הכרזות אין ידיעה ברורה מי היה האמן שצייר, מכיוון שאינן חתומות; אולם כיים יסוד סביר להניח שהה זה אגרובצינץ, החתום על חלק מכרזות בית הקולנוע. שמות הכוכבים הראשיים צוירו על פי רוב ביד. שיטה זו נוצרה להכבלים את שמחורות כאות מדריכית לשמות הפרטים האחרים אשר הודפסו ביד סדרי דפוס מאות כלם סמורית סטנדרטיית. ציורי אותיות אלה נסרקו ונחברה הבדלי הסמגנונה הרדים ביניהן. לאחר מכן נתחחו סרי האופי העיקריים של אותיות אלה על מנת שישמשו בסים לעיצוב פונט דיגיטלי מחושב. בשלב הבא העברה הנתונים לתכנה מתאימה ונוצבה האות. הציוב המחודש הוסף אות זו לפעילה וניתן להשתמש בה כמחשב מסינטוש.

Font and poster design by **Oded Ezer** at the **Bezalel Academy of Art and Design, Jerusalem** 1998

Poster featuring Eden typeface
1998

5.03 inches

6.31 inches

7.6 inches

8.88 inches

10.17 inches

1.18 inches

2.46 inches

4.4.2003

225.75 mm

258.375 mm

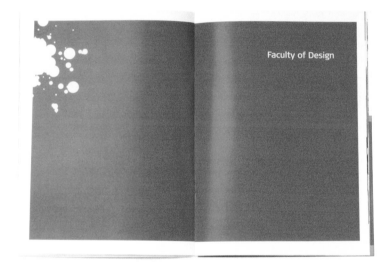

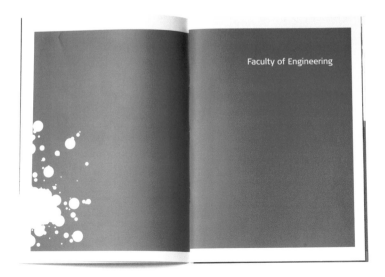

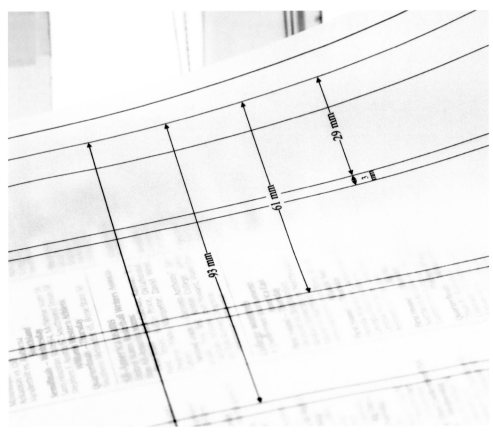

Editorial design for Firma
a magazine for media, television and advertising
Designed in cooperation with Shimon Zandhaus, 1999

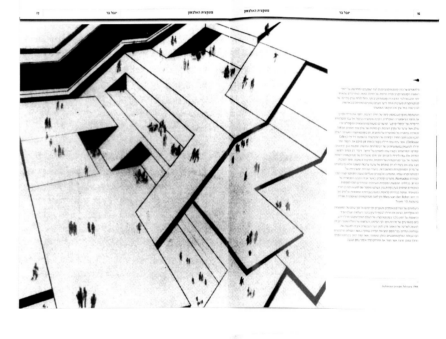

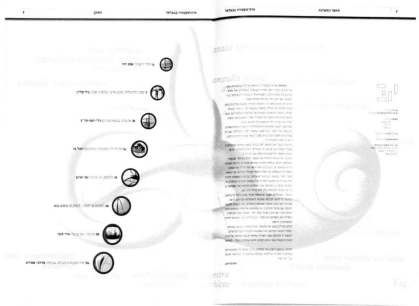

3D Studies
Photographed by Idan Gil

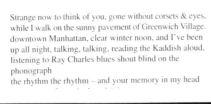

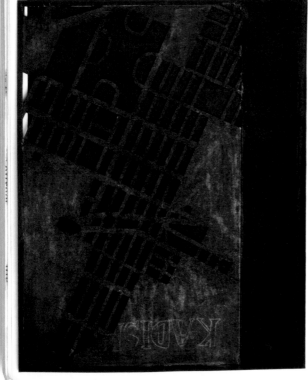

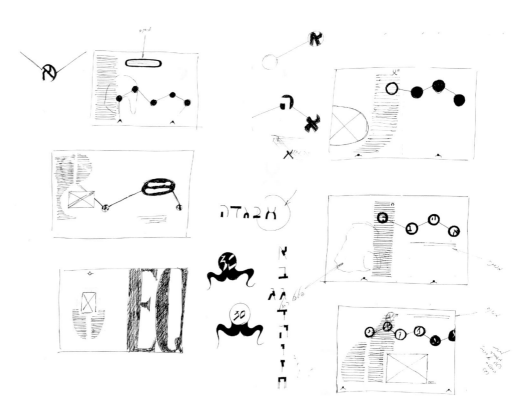

Editorial design sketches
1995

**Sketches of page numbers
for a magazine spread**
1995

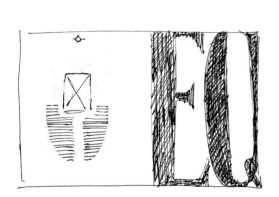

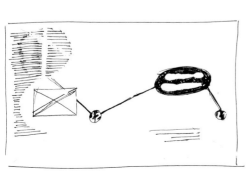

"Ok" logo sketches
1994

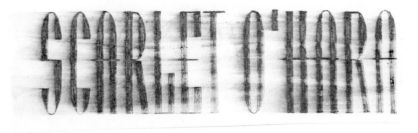

"Rewind" poster
A reaction to the assassination of Prime
Minister Yitzhak Rabin, 1995

Logo sketches
1995

Cc
Logo for student design exhibition at the Bezalel Gallery, Jerusalem, 1998

Lily
Logo for an art exhibition at the Efrat Gallery Tel Aviv, 2004

Larin
Logo for jewelry designer Gregory Larin, Tel Aviv, 2005

Globes
Logo update for a daily financial newspaper, 1999

Muzik
Logo for Muzik School - a music and productions school, Tel Aviv, 2005

Itai Asher Meir
Logo for a magician, 2008

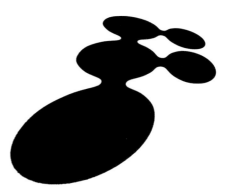

Dj
Logo for a Dj school, 2002

Floor
Logo for a club, 1997

Ego
Logo for a café and bookshop, 1997

לילי עזר ציירת ומורה לאמנות פלסטית
רחוב הנוטרים 29 נוה הברון, זכרון יעקב 30900
טל. 04-6399732
leezer@netvision.net.il

Business Cards

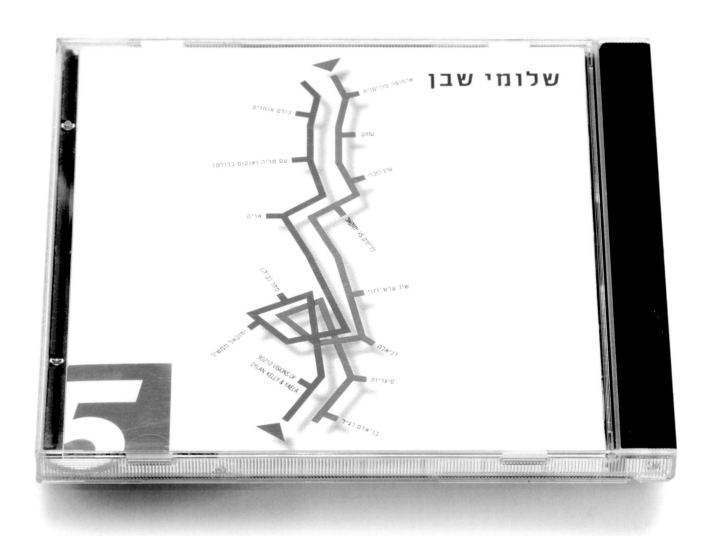

"Shlomi Shaban"
CD cover for an Israeli pop musician, 2000

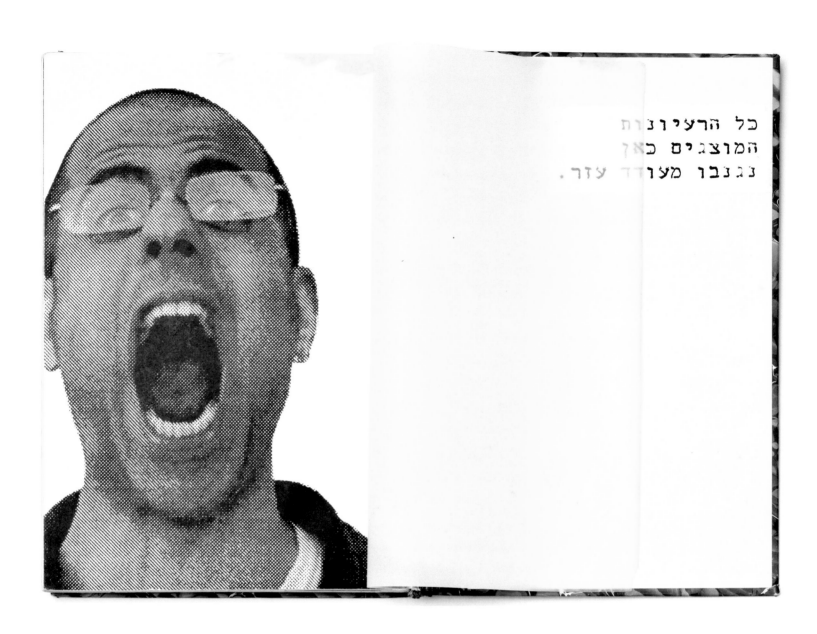

כל הרעיונות
המוצגים כאן
נגנבו מעודד עזר.

Self-portrait

Oded at 3

3D Study "In these studies, I didn't use letters because I was just concentrating on structure, but later I used the results on letters. I wanted to see if I could create something meaningful with something as simple as newspaper clippings. I thought using information in another way might add something to the composition. I wanted to take something – this is very common printed matter – and turn it into something very poetic."

Givataiym Sinking This project was inspired by an exhibition called "The End of the World" which featured works dealing with the Apocalypse theme. Oded did not participated in the exhibition, however, he was inspired by it and drew a sketch on the topic illustrating the Hebrew word for "the end" drowning in a puddle of oil. One day when driving by the logo of his home town Gi-vataiym, he had the idea of applying the concept of this logo to his apocalyptic sketch. The dark and pessimistic yet comic-esque result was an ironic reversion of the friendly white original standing in a flowerbed. This work which was never realized for a specific reason was later bought by Oded's colleague who thought it was a ingenious individual item.

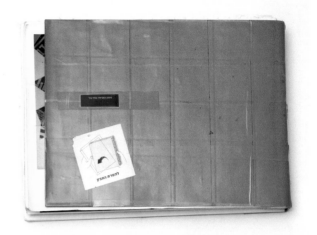

Details from personal sketchbook
2000

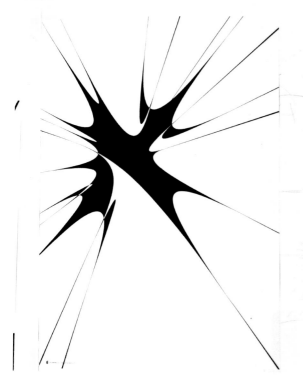

Details from personal sketchbook
2001

"Telepathy"
Poster for a parapsychological
event, 1993

"Crying dove"
A political statement for Yediot
Tikshoret newspaper, 1992

All You Need Is Cash
1992

Poster commenting on the sell-out of the rights to Beatles songs. In 1985 Michael Jackson outbid Yoko Ono and Paul McCartney at a cost of 47.5 million Dollars.

3D studies	Illustration of Oded's student flat
1994	1995

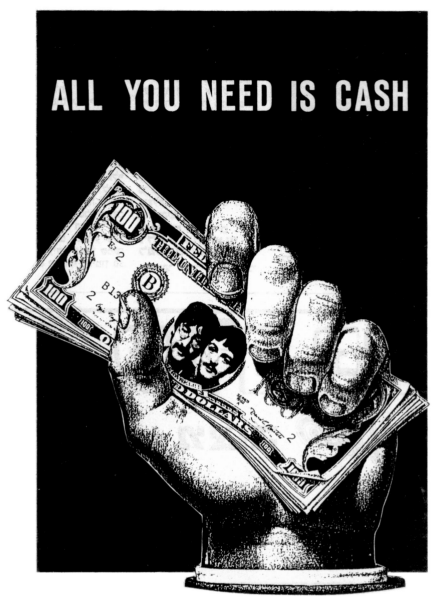

**Illustrations and layout designs
for school newspapers**
1987–1990

**Illustrations and layout designs
for school newspapers**
1987 - 1990

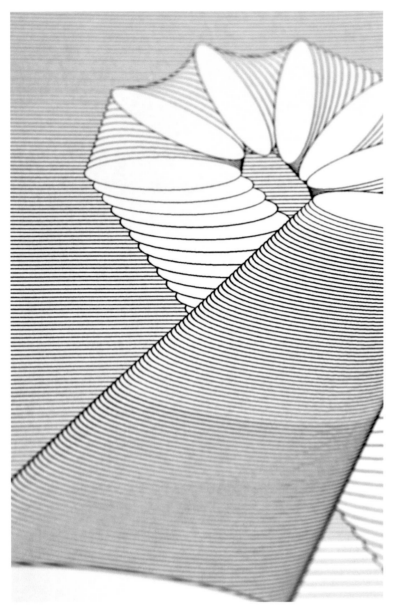

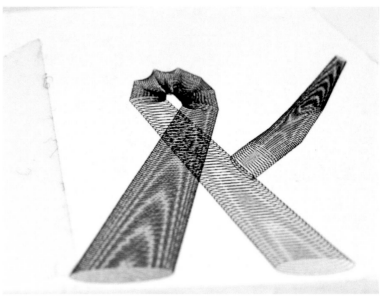

Details from personal sketchbook
2001

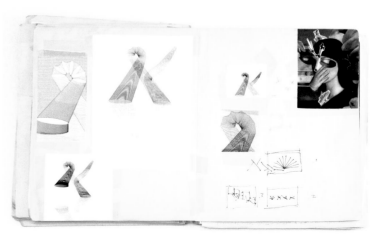

85

Details from personal sketchbook
2002

Graphic Work   Oded Ezer

Between
the Letters
On Growing

by Kitty Bolhöfer

∞ "There was always a big gap between what I felt graphic design should be about and what I was told graphic design is."

When reminiscing about childhood places, we tend to envision enchanted locations where colours are always brighter and the smell in the air is always sweeter – even if we grew up in a prefab colony next to the highway. When Oded Ezer talks about his home-town Ramat Gan, it seems that there is no need to sugarcoat facts. The sunny city close to Tel Aviv translates as "Garden Heights" and as such it offers a wealth of lush parks, gardens and tree-lined streets. Back in the seventies, the historic "Elite" brand, a famous local chocolate and coffee manufacturer, ran a factory there, so a delicious aroma filled the air. Despite all these charms, Oded acknowledges that as a child he perceived the buildings, the street signs and the way people dressed as rather bland and gray; thus his overall impression of the city is characterised by mediocrity. This is not a sign of bitterness towards the past; it is just more proof that Oded Ezer is anyone but everyone else. As so often in his life, he simply did things differently. Instead of glorifying his childhood memories in the present, he had daydreams of a future with brighter colours and new shapes for buildings and street signs. In the meantime, he has realized that he is the one who has to make those changes; his dissatisfaction became an impetus that pointed the way to his vocation.

Not simply accepting the given facts but challenging them instead has become a leitmo-tif for Oded Ezer. To break viewing habits at a time and in a place where one's stomping ground is largely shielded from the rest of the world's cultural influences, however, takes a great deal of courage. Growing up in a small country without any sort of new visual culture around and no global communication tools such as the Internet, where do you get inspiration? Where do you get the confidence to try alternatives? Looking back, it was probably this very stage of insulation that over the years made him develop extraordinary designing skills and completely new ways of thinking, not to mention persistency. The little boy whose eyes were glued to anything with words on it – be it signs or magazines – always tried to understand why letters looked the way they did. His questioning, the yearning to learn more was like a seed planted in his brain that constantly grew; the more it was challenged by boundaries set by teachers and working life, the stronger an entity it became. Even today, like a seedling, it is far from fully-grown. It regularly needs to be watered with knowledge that established methodologies cannot provide; Oded finds the right nourishment in his experimentation. In return, the plant spits out little offspring every once in a while, letter-like pollen that venture forth to do what the young boy in the chocolate-scented town dreamt of: to change the look of people's worlds.

Between the Letters
Inexhaustible creator of letters and alphabets

by Cinzia Ferrara

IT REALLY IS A SHAME THAT ONE MUST LEAF THROUGH THE PAGES OF CHILDREN'S BOOKS TO BE TRULY AMAZED BY POP-UPS – TWISTING AND TURNING, FOLDING, SWELLING, JUMPING UP TO CREATE INCREDIBLE BUILDINGS.

One follows the adventures of their heroes, as they make their way through fragmentary landscapes they are called on to cross – through forests and valleys, in and out of tiny houses, castles and ravines, past dinosaurs and dragons, through ocean beds with octopuses and sperm whales, and across imaginary spaces. The shapes of these tales' heroes rise up from the pages of the books in which they dwell, like the memory of some unpunished crime, as if they too feel the same strong sense of wonder that we do. They spring into action to tread the surfaces of the pages once inhabited by their bodies. In some contexts, the passage from two to three dimensional landscapes, i.e. from a flat to a pop-up world, which is naturally more similar to the one we actually inhabit, continues to amaze us. It is still unexpected, something that nearly always takes us by surprise, catches us off guard. Luckily for us there is no danger, unlike in the case of A. Square, the heroic star of Flatland, a science fiction novella written by the English reverend Edwin A. Abbott in 1884. When he declares publically that he is able to see worlds not in one or two but even in three dimensions, thanks to a magic sphere, A. Square (and all those like him) are thrown into jail. He ends his days in prison charged with being completely off his head.

Yet such concerns barely come up in the safe world of typography, which essentially tends to deal with a flat dimension. The elements leave ink and paper marks, adding no more layers other than a barely perceivable extra thickness. No one is surprised when this is later reduced to nothing, relegating the typographic elements, consigning the characters, to the flatness of a one-dimensional space.

There is one person, however, who is not content just to leave the letters as they are, to sit back looking at them. He is someone not at all convinced that characters should be merely a question of width and length, with no regard for thickness. If only he would stop and realise that letters are, as we all know, meant for a two-dimensional space. Then, perhaps, he would stop trying to imagine that they have their own nature, one that only a few chosen visionaries are able to see, hidden inside, nestled at the heart of each different glyph. There are plenty who disagree with him and simply trust first impressions, thinking they represent reality. This holds for the sailors described in the first few pages of Flatland:

> "They traverse your seas and discern some distant island or coast lying on the horizon. The far-off land may have bays, forelands, angles in and out to any number and extent; yet at a distance you see none of these (unless indeed your sun shines bright upon them revealing the projections and retirements by means of light and shade), nothing but a grey unbroken line upon the water." [1]

[1] **Flatland: A Romance of Many Dimensions** (1884) by Edwin Abbott.

Oded Ezer sails those same seas, but when he sights land he knows only too well that behind that "grey unbroken line upon the water," there lies a three-dimensional reality. This is the very same reality with which he imbues his letters, offering them the chance to inhabit a spatial realm rather than simply dwelling on a flat plane.

He is someone who has expectations for these letters, inventing completely new contexts and spaces for them, moving away from the white page, where we have become accustomed to seeing them as anonymous workers in the service of a text. He is someone who has begun to think of a place for his letters where, like living creatures, they can come to life, grow, reproduce, and even eventually die. It is a place where they can be manufactured, like any other industrial product, only to become obsolete, as is so often eventually the case with everyday objects. It is a place where they can take the shape of animals, hybrid versions of their forms, as if grotesquely grafted onto the glyphs to form a wholly surreal Bestiary. The many different dimensions that Oded Ezer has come up with for his letters mean that they all fit into many different lives, that may be as short as a butterfly's or as unreal as those inhabited by our dreams. For any reference to this dreamlike dimension is not entirely accidental when it comes to talking about Oded Ezer, given that, metaphorically speaking, his experiments take place in the dead of night. Then, he is free to design, push back the boundaries, free himself from the constraints of functional and ergonomic limitations, from the rational considerations of his day job when he works (with great success) in his Tel Aviv studio. His daily life sees him working mainly as a type-designer for companies and institutions, designing customer and corporate fonts to help forge a strong identity for them. As well, he works as a graphic designer, busying himself with the design of logos and posters, where the results of his nocturnal experiments on lettering sometimes get the chance to put in an appearance. They are two completely different worlds, one feeding market demand, the other nurturing an unquenchable thirst for knowledge, a need to keep on experimenting. Perhaps, or rather, almost certainly, these two worlds end up as mutually beneficial channels of communication, each flowing into the other, at once representing the "real" and the "dream"-world dimensions of this young Israeli type designer.

Oded Ezer adores continually crossing over the threshold of the seemingly level world of typography, where he discovers, by looking through his magnifying glass, that what had once appeared to be contained in just one flat layer, in reality is not so flat after all. If you look closely at the letters of the alphabet, there might just be a whole new three-dimensional world out there, where the unruly letters rise up, refusing to take their position lying down. They leap off the page, fly through space, climb up the walls, and even take shape in materials that have little to do with thick jet-black ink or the intangible pixels of our computer screens. They form in materials like green plasticine, black rubber, red enamel, transparent silicon, white paper, yellow clay, silvery metal, or dark and porous sponge. In this way, his unusual letters end up looking quite different, although no matter what features they are given, they still retain their true identities in some way. For, in reality, they are little bodies, with their own material consistency, bound by the weight of their own inertia. Yet, they also have their very own shape, smell, consistency, colour, and texture −all of which means that we can bring them into our own material world, where we can not only see them but almost make eye contact with and feel for them.

What makes Oded Ezer so very special is not only that he has given us this stunning experimental world, but he has also challenged us to take a new look at typography. He wants us to see it as never before, in an unusual way, almost transversally as it were, purging it of a former reputation promoted by teachers. The twenty-six letters we are so used to seeing, that we barely pay attention to, should finally get the attention they really deserve, free from the prejudices of old and open to experimentation. All you need to do is to leaf through some of Ezer's sketch albums and you can find thousands of different ideas for designs, ranging from superimposed embryonic letter forms, to compositions using those very same letters, some of which may be rigid, geometric and three dimensional. Others are soft, bendy and organic, so that they move over the surface or are repeated over and over, adding a kinetic dimension to the work. Or you can try taking a look at the plastic models he builds on his own in his studio, using the most diverse and unlikely materials. Or you can study the posters he has designed, where the way his letters are placed on the page gives true meaning to their positioning.

What is more, it is not just our visual sense that is gratified, but all the other ones too. Every receptive fibre of our bodies is drawn to feel his world of typography, where letters are created by him in such an unusual way. The unique and sometimes somewhat unfathomable way he works is possibly easier to understand if viewed by analysing a series of elements. One of which concerns his method of research which draws on work in traditional spheres of typography and graphic design, going right back to its origins, and which, even though it lies at the heart of his work, seems to be pretty much relegated to the back bench by him. At the same time, he gets well away from the obvious choices, and can be seen to prefer an eclectic mix of input from other disciplines and art forms, things that truly grab his interest, so that he is able to draw unbiased inspiration from the diverse worlds of music, architecture, design, and even from the worlds of biology and science. It is as if he would mock all those who would rather compartmentalise their subjects, by deliberately breaking down barriers and creating new hybrid forms of art. It is precisely this approach that makes Ezer something of a beacon, leading the way, shining his light onto flat hidden corners where none have looked before, as if armed with a special pass allowing him access into all scholastic disciplines. He pilfers key concepts from them and brings them back as ideas to be suggested and transformed into his work as a type designer, creator of real or imaginary letters, whether these are in ink or any other material.

> "A letter is something that came up from culture, it is an artificial sign for something which has a meaning and long history behind it. What I'm trying to do is to understand this process of creating and re-shaping this cultural element."

What is more, the forms he comes up with for every letter are various. By no means all of these are exactly functional in terms of reading and writing, many have been designed simply to occupy a sort of no man's land, balancing between the world of experimental typography and artistic expression. Yet, in spite of this, such steps on his journey of design are by no means any less important.

Ezer designs his letters not for the flat white page but rather for the empty field – i.e. the empty space where he is free from the constraints of his day job to explore new horizons, where the light shining over the shadows of these tiny bodies reveals their hidden depths, as well as every other detail of their shapes, outing their three-dimensional nature.

This is how the creatures for his Biotypography transform into tiny unknown living beings, their bodies barely hinting at the presence of the alphabet letters they represent: transparent wings, tails and ears, sprout from them along with long spindly legs or arched stingers.

Then there are other tiny beings such as those in his Typosperma project where the sperm take on the features of small transgenic embryos with typographic information implanted in their DNA, not wholly recognisable since they are still in the process of growing, invisible to the naked eye – something you can only see in the lab with highly specialised instruments.

Or there are the creatures you can see in his Tybrid letters which are not so much animate as inanimate, taking the form of household objects so as to resemble revolving office chairs, coat hangers, fork prongs, and even worn-out old padded couches, that are losing bits of their straw stuffing and sprouting metal springs.

Then there are these indistinct rough-hewn forms, like stuffed and covered dried-up black-gloss ink, piled together on top of one another on the floor of a room, and which, if left to their own devices, can be seen crawling straight up walls to conquer a coiled third dimension.

It is the same third dimension as that of the tiny cutout letters that lift off the page, printed for a compact disc of the Israeli composer Arie Shapira. They become equally expressive, like his harsh, dramatic and yet torn music. His letters move across an imaginary stage, playing the parts they have been given by an author who, somewhat tyrannically, has decided not only their roles but their destinies. This is why they know how to make themselves small, as silent miniature signs, able to keep out of things and miss their meaning, just like they do in the poster for Stami and Klumi, which could be roughly translated into English as something like Mr. Unimportant and Mr. Nothing, provocations created by the Israeli poet Yona Volach. In keeping with the words of the poem, the letters are made out of chewing gum masticated by the designer, then discharged and smeared on the page to make long threads that stretch out and pile up on one another, so that each glyph is superimposed over the next. For Ezer's letters are also able to suffer, and show that they do not just provoke feelings but also feel them for themselves; like the tortured letters he makes out of rubber and then mercilessly ties to pylons leaving them hanging in space, silent in their pain. His nailed letters also show a sense of suffering, their shapes created by sticking them to invisible threads making rows of nails. These letters were created in a tribute to the Israeli graphic designer David Tartakover, which inevitably leads us to think of the nails of scatter bombs that release their contents on explosion, as if there needed to be any reminder of the terrible pain and suffering which these bring when they are detonated.

"All the heights and depths and breadths of tangible and natural things - landscapes, sunsets, the scent of hay, the hum of bees, the beauty which belongs to eyelids (and is falsely ascribed to eyes); all the immeasurable emotions, and motions of the human mind, to which there seems no bound; ugly and terrible and mysterious thoughts and things, as well as beautiful- all are compassed, restrained, ordered, in a trifling jumble of letters. Twenty-six signs!"

So wrote the English typographer Francis Meynell in 1923, who, with his innate sense of poetry, coupled with the ability to dream a little, was able to see, with great realism, the great potential that lay beyond the shape of each lead character. He saw that this same tiny army of soldiers could work as a team to transform spoken words into print, teaching the Muse, who already knew how to talk, not only how to write but even how to publish what she wrote.

I believe that Oded Ezer has brought Meynell's vision to its full capitulation, first taking on board his lessons and then even taking them a step further, thanks to the broad architecture of his approach which crosses disciplines of all shapes and sizes with the casual ease of a great designer, one who has always found it easy to tackle two-dimensional systems of representation and yet who is equally at home with 3D models, truly fascinated by the impalpable world of ideas, seeing these in the measure with which they can later become solid realities, bringing them to life in this material world, carving out an all new space for his letters, while at the same time managing to seek out new horizons to aim for in his research.

Ezer often moves in two different worlds, coming and going between the two with the ease of a needle pulling a thread, and binding the two tightly together: blending the real with the unreal, work and research, flat and raised, legible and illegible, pixel and material, and even traditional and innovative.

Ezer has learned to live with his dual nature, one which leads him to be in continual contradiction even when it comes to traditional Hebrew script, on the one hand giving it all his attention, on the other attempting to renew it from within, openly betraying it from above, paying attention to other alphabets like the Latin one.

This is what has happened in 2002, when, taking as a starting point the Sys font created by his Italian friend and colleague Fabrizio Schiavi, Ezer came up variations on a theme for the Hebrew alphabet which he called Systeza. This has resulted in both interesting and highly valid forms for both writing systems. The letters are completely different from one another, both in terms of their origin and form, yet at the same time Schiavi's font and Ezer's Hebrew mutations still have something in common; one feature is that both have a strongly geometric look to them, especially given that they are born out of a prototype for a bitmap, another is that they have managed to make the structure of the Hebrew alphabet far more contemporary, so that the letters, which are quite geometric, are also drawn with thickset horizontal lines, tied together by thinner vertical ones. In this way, through his collaboration with Schiavi, Ezer has been able to open a dialogue between two different cultures in the world of typography, in a design project which takes the idea of hybrids one step further, opening it out to cross geographical borders in a way that would surely have delighted Galileo Galilei, himself a great fan of the alphabet as can be seen from his words.

"Of all the truly great inventions, what great mind came up with a means of communicating his deepest thoughts to any other person, talking at any distance or over any great stretch of time? To be able to talk with those who are in the Indies, or to leave messages for those not yet even born, and who may not yet appear here for another good thousand and ten years or so? And with what ease? With the simple device of a mere twenty or so characters on a page."

There is a picture of Oded as a child sitting on a table with a few things in front of him, a few sheets of paper, a pencil with a rubber on the end, a toy lorry. In the background, you can make out the wallpaper with smiling bears, flowering shrubs and trees and tiny houses which are arranged in a pattern that covers the whole wall. The same pattern seems to cover the table, in focus in this picture. The colours have faded to a brownish colour, making the photo look older than it really is. If you look carefully, you can also see that he has an intense expression revealing a combination of wonder and that innate capacity that small children have to be readily captivated, staring rudely at anyone and anything, refusing to avert their gaze, in the same way that Oded does whenever he poses for a photo. You can still find the same expression in the grown-up Oded, although these days there is the added filter of a pair of black-framed glasses, which he now has to wear. It is also the same expression which, through his work, he is hoping to obtain from us, with this funny cheeky approach, like a modern day Munari of the graphics world, able at once to challenge his own work and to remember not to take himself too seriously. It is like when he has his photo taken wearing a lab coat, daring us to rise to his implicit challenge, carefully attempting to extract his bendy silicon letters from his nostrils or pulling at them as if they were growths to be removed from his body.

Oded Ezer, the grown-up child is only too aware of his use of all the tricks and tools at his disposal, with no holds barred. He is undeniably a designer of his time, tied to tradition whilst at the same time looking forward to imaginary and magnificent frontiers. These edges are both real and utopian, concrete and invisible, in that dizzy and fantastic world of letters in which we would all like to believe – just as he does – so that we can also lose ourselves there with equal wonder.

English translation by Alison Bron

Between the Letters
A Guided Tour through the Typographer's Galaxy

A conversation between Oded Ezer and Kitty Bolhöfer

MAYBE TIME PASSES MORE SLOWLY IN ODED EZER'S UNIVERSE. IN ADDITION TO DIVIDING HIS WAKING HOURS INTO DAY SHIFTS AS A COMMERCIAL TYPOGRAPHER AND TYPE DESIGNER AND NIGHT SHIFTS AS A TYPOGRAPHIC EXPERIMENTALIST STRIVING TO CHANGE THE WORLD, AWARD-WINNING ODED EZER IS ALSO A MEMBER OF THE ICD (ISRAEL COMMUNITY OF DESIGNERS). BESIDES TEACHING TYPOGRAPHY, TYPE DESIGN AND GRAPHIC DESIGN, HE HAS TAKEN ON THE CHALLENGE OF BEING A CARING HUSBAND AND FATHER TO HIS BABY SON. SOMEHOW, HE HAS FOUND THE TIME TO GIVE US A VERBAL TOUR THROUGH HIS TYPOGRAPHICAL UNIVERSE AND ITS EVOLUTIONARY HISTORY.

Why did you choose the name The Typographer's Guide to the Galaxy for your book? I'm aware of the fact that in "real" life – just as in Douglas Adams's science fiction comedy The Hitchhiker's Guide to the Galaxy – there is no prescription for a true creative process or personal progression. I treat it as a chance for other people to get on a ride to the inside of my mind – my inner typo galaxy, its landscape and some datumpoints of the creative process – a ride that, I hope, will be not only useful, but also fun.

What are the brightest stars in the constellation of your galaxy? Where do they lead to? Well… I have to say that I feel so lucky to find the time for experimentation and development; that kind of play is actually the brightest star here. Exhibitions, publications, accolades, talks, meeting with interesting people all over the world – these are all wonderful, but only "side effects". I can tell you that even without all these benefits, I would still continue to investigate because it makes me feel alive. Where am I going from here? I will be hitchhiking to discover a new galaxy, of course (laughs).

What does typography mean to you and how does this meaning affect your work? I find typography a powerful tool. A written word is both the content and the object that carries it. Is it a "thing" or a "symbol of a thing"? Or both? I relate to these places because, for me, when I make a circle made of hair, it is a circle made of hair. But if I write the word "circle" in a manner that makes it look like hair, it opens up a whole new field for interpretation. And this is what I like about typography. This is why I'm a typographer. In works such as the Typo Mythologies project, the Biotypography or the Typosperma projects, it must be the possibility of playing with my own and other people's perceptions about culture and life through typography that makes this medium so attractive to me. I use letters, words and paragraphs in order to achieve this, simply because I have found out that it is much easier for me to deliver ideas through these elements than, let's say, music or poetry.

When you started creating your galaxy, you were one of the first typographers to develop letters into the third dimension. What is the situation now? Let me tell you about something interesting I recently found on the Internet: there are now two guys in Estonia who sell three-dimensional typefaces. They create fonts using a computer program and sell them as Photoshop files on their website. I feel that in a way, this is the end of a revolution; it is amazing how 3D digital or material-based typography, which was quite rare – if not esoteric – only a few years ago, has become so popular and imaginable now. The kind of typography that I dreamt of has become reality. My intuition tells me that now it is time to go ahead into the future, to twenty or even fifty years from now, and to run away from what has become mainstream.

Do you consider this development to be slow or quick? It depends on how you look at it. When you think about how conceivable it is now to come up with such a concept, it seems that this development took very long. But when I remember how the typography world was when I just started – and I can give you no more than three names of people who were pioneers in this field in the last century – it happened very quickly.

You took a completely new path, off the beaten track and you paved it for others. What enabled you to do that? Was it simply creativity? I don't really know. It's definitely not just creativity because everybody is kind of creative. It is probably the ability to put a great deal of effort into self-produced work. When I talk to other graphic designers, they sometimes don't understand how I find the time to experiment. People don't understand how someone can work so hard on something that does not pay off immediately, because we are all struggling with everyday life and everyone has to make a living. I guess that is my main strength: taking time for my experiments. I have the need to do something that challenges the perception of what typography is.

How did your different perception of typography come about? I grew up in Ramat Gan, a typical Israeli city, in the seventies. I remember that as a child I looked around, and everything seemed so gray – although it was a very sunny place! It probably wasn't really gray; that was just my experience of the city. That feeling of mediocrity was disappointing. So, as a child, I always daydreamed that something would happen to change the look of the letters on the street signs, the look of the buildings and the way people dressed.

Another kind of frustration was with words – and that is something that anyone who deals with the philosophy of the language feels. It's the problem that words only name objects but they do not include them. The word "chair" is just a general symbol that has nothing to do with a real chair. In a way, I felt that this was wrong because it removed a very sensual part from our language.

How can you re-introduce that lost dimension to your work?   By thinking about letters as living creatures; thinking about letters as humans; combining letters with letters and letters with objects; distorting, folding, rounding letters or parts in them; cutting letters out of paper or cutting parts of letters; recreating letters from other materials and using techniques and methodologies from other disciplines such as biology, chemistry, architecture, anthropology, etc.

But as a teenager you didn't only deal with the visual aspects of writing ...   No, you could say that I was on the other side of words. In high school, I played the guitar, so my friends and I had a rock band and I got involved in songwriting. Later, during my time in the military, I went on to write poems without music. I dealt with poetry a lot back then.

How do military training and poetry go together?   Well, Israel is such a small country that they need each and every one of us. Thus, the army aims to motivate all kinds of people and supports their interests. I was in a special artists' program where part of the time soldiers could deal with what they were interested in and could pass that knowledge on to the community. My group was stationed in the desert, where we taught children art. The other part was regular military training. I was sort of "lucky" though, because I was wounded during training. Nothing dramatic; I fell on my weapon and dislocated my arm, but it took me out for about half a year. Since I couldn't fight, my commander assigned me to design stage settings and layouts for posters and flyers.

What does the Israeli army design stage settings for?   They have lots of dance and music events, which are an integral part of Israeli culture. The most famous and established singers of the country started their careers in the army and that is also where I started out as a graphic designer. Before, I only had a musical background. I did graphics when I was a teenager; I was involved in the layout and design of our school newspaper. But I never considered doing that as a profession. In high school, I realized that I wasn't talented enough to become a musician and that I am quite competitive! I wanted to find a field where I could feel stronger and deliver things without simplifying them, and I found it in graphic design. Right after military service, I went to the Bezalel Academy for Arts and Design. Actually, the two stages overlapped. I took the entrance exams still wearing my uniform. I was kind of in a hurry. Now that I had found what I wanted to do, I didn't want to waste any more time.

How did you experience graphic design at the academy?   I always have mixed feelings when I look back. One thing is for sure though: in the early nineties, the Bezalel Academy was the place to study graphic design in Israel because there was no real competition around. This school had the best teachers and the best students; I was very lucky to be in the same class with brilliant people, but sometimes I felt like it was too intense and competitive. It was not only tough; I was not convinced that the things most of my teachers told me were the only things to learn about graphic design. I didn't have the guts to say exactly what I wanted because I was not as brave as I am today. As a student, I just wanted to understand everything and I wanted to be praised.

What where you missing in your studies?   The thing was, I came from a high school centred on the arts and I used to have all kinds of artists such as actors, dancers, painters, jazz and classical musicians around me. The environment was so full of different aspects of art, and this was something I missed at the design academy. Everybody talked only about graphic design; no one took the time to recognise recent developments in – let's say – product design, movies, fashion or dance. I thought that was wrong.

Nowadays you give lectures yourself. Do you do things differently in your teaching? I hope so. I think I'm considered quite strange – as a teacher as well as a graphic designer or typographer. In the beginning, I taught only traditional typography and editorial design. But in the last two years, there was a great change: suddenly I was invited to teach experimental typography. I guess the Academy got used to my ideas. It was just a matter of time.

So you also became a pioneer in teaching. I cannot take the entire credit myself, though. My own teachers were also pioneers in their field. I guess that is because Israel is such a young country; you have to be a pioneer here. Improvising is part of our culture. In Europe, everything is already established, so improvising is not really considered a value, but in Israel it is! Sometimes it is a substitute for doing something right (laughs). In that way, I must admit that I am very much an Israeli.

With this improvisatory aspect of your work and the frustration with how the city looked when you were younger, why did you never experiment with street art? There was no such scene here when I was growing up in the seventies and eighties. Street culture didn't enter Israeli cities until the late nineties. It eventually came with Jewish immigrants mainly from the former USSR but also from Europe. The Internet changed the situation a lot, too. Suddenly, we were connected to the rest of the world and it became easy for people to adopt American and European styles in real time. Now, through the media, we are much more exposed to what is happening in other countries, so the visual culture here is changing very fast. The revolution simply arrived in Israel a few years later.

How did this change affect your work as a graphic designer? The Internet was a very important tool for me. I just started to work and develop my experiments around 2000, when it was already here. For the first time, I was sitting in my home in Givatayim and was able to reach out to the whole world! I made a poster in Hebrew and was able to send it over to my friends in Europe, and suddenly people started to know me. It was so easy! So in my experimental work, there are some similarities to the philosophy of street art: I address the public without any client being involved in the process and I also suggest new applications. I add another angle to a word and sometimes make its real meaning less important. The difference is that I always start with traditional letterforms. I don't call it art; it is always typo even if it is sometimes too hard to read. If my work is comparable at all, then it is to the pioneers of street art. My work has different roots; I am focused on finding out what I can do with letters as such. To me, street art is a brother to my work – but not the father.

Who is the father? There were several: Edward Ruscha for example. He is a painter, but he painted words: he is the perfect balance between conceptual art and pop art. In this way, he influenced me a great deal. And I am just in the middle; between conceptual art and typography. I think he was a pioneer who opened the door for people like me. Not by technical means, but by the philosophy behind his work, although he would never call it philosophy. Another direct influence was Studio Dumbar in the mid-eighties or Takenobu Igarashi with his letter statues. Back then, they were the only people who dealt with aspects of 3D typo that I knew.

What attracts you so strongly to three-dimensional typography? It is always a surprise to see because you don't expect letters to be three-dimensional. Something that deeply impressed me in the early days was a small pamphlet called Dimensional Typography: Words in Space by J. Abbott Miller in the mid-nineties that a friend brought back for me from the USA. Actually, it was an experiment in 2D typo using 3D computer programs. I had never seen anything like it before; Miller used product design methods on letters in times when all 3D programming was still in its infancy. The book showed letters rotating in a computer program and they looked like strange typo objects. Everything he did was computerized; nothing was ever done by hand. I think that was the first time that my brain started to run very quickly. It took me two more years – until after I graduated – to understand what I needed to do: to decide that I was going to devote at least half of my time to experiments and to see how typography can benefit from technology.

Why did it take you so long to realize that?   Well, it was the opposite of what I had been taught at school. I had to get used to the thought, because we had been taught that we couldn't combine two methods; it was considered contradictory. If you did typography, you couldn't do illustration! Now it is very common, but in those times it was a no-no. You had to decide whether you wanted to be a typographer, a cartoonist or an illustrator, but in this little book they combined science, technology and typo!

After two years of getting used to that thought, how did you finally approach the new idea?   I realized that in order to do something revolutionary, it would take time and I knew that I wouldn't be happy working for clients only because then I would always have to subordinate my ideas to their demands. Then again, it was the only way to earn money. Eventually, I decided that I needed a firm base so I scheduled my work on experimental, "non-profit items" for night time and called them NPI. I am a graphic designer, after all, so I felt that I needed a logo for that. In the beginning I stamped every experimental piece with it. It really helped me in my early stage, because nobody had told me that this kind of work was a legitimate process. But I needed to label it somehow.

When working experimentally, who or what do you bear in mind? Your audience? The novelty aspect? Your own development as a typo artist?   It is usually the concept's narrative that I bear in mind. When at my best, I succeed not looking sideways, but by following the narrative path in a sincere way. I try not to mix my ego or my old perceptions, nor to interfere in the process with down-to-earth demands.

What is your aim when working on a design?   My first aim is to play and enjoy as much as I can (laughs). My basic philosophies are very simple… design should be fun, not tiring. Try to treat any problem as a challenge. Daydream. Sketch. Never throw away any sketch or piece of work, no matter how stupid and pathetic it is; 'bad' ideas now, can be brilliant solutions in the future. Design should be easy to produce; if something becomes too complicated, simply avoid that direction. Use simple and cheap materials and techniques. Amuse yourself. Always listen to other people; never let anyone else decide for you. Unless you have a real reason, work with black and white only. Unless you have a real reason, work on your own. Don't look at graphic design books (including this one) for inspiration when you are short of new ideas; instead, take a long walk or meditate. Adopt other people's methodologies, not their style. Be obsessive. Be generous. Be as honest as you possibly can.

How do you find the materials? While designing? In everyday life situations? What comes first, the material or the idea for the project?   Sometimes, as in the unimportant & nothing poster, it was the material – chewing gum in this case – that led me to action. Also in the Tortured letters and the Temporary type series, it was materials I had found – strings, industrial rubber and industrial air conditioner filters – that played the main role in developing the typographic phenomena from a very early stage of the design. But in other cases, such as the Plastica, the Biotypography or the Now projects, where I used materials such as plasticine, fimo or nails, it could be that the material followed the idea.

How do you feel about your corporate work now that you have established yourself as a designer?   My view on that has changed. When I first started my experiments, I thought that my commercial work was a waste of time. However, if I didn't enjoy it, I wouldn't do it at all.

Was it the type of work that changed or your attitude?   Both. I now appreciate commercial work more and also, the market has approached me. Furthermore, over the years I have become a better commercial designer. I don't see it as a hassle anymore (laughs).

Do you feel that you are also given more freedom now that you have a reputation?
Absolutely. Still, there are some parameters that a commercial graphic designer has to take into consideration. On the one hand, it is the business he designs for, but on the other hand, it is the audience that will buy the company's product. The third aspect is the quality of his work. I cannot design anything extraordinary for the Israeli market because there are only few hundred thousand potential buyers at stake and companies here keep their audience strongly in mind. This is because the latter is usually very limited since Israel is so small. The problem is that you have to consider the fact that at the end of the day, you have very limited number of clients and you don't want to make anyone angry. It is about balancing all these aspects. That is why it is very hard to do any breakthrough commercial design in Israel.

Don't you think that a breakthrough is hard in any country?   I don't know. Well, I guess it is always hard to be very creative whether there are thousands or millions of buyers involved. But then again, you can be very creative within these restrictions. I always try to use what I have learned from my experiments and the work I have already done for other clients. Sometimes experiments even turn into commercial work. Sometimes clients approach me because I do have an open mind and they trust that I won't use it against them. They know that I am very responsible towards graphical work because I know that once it is out, it will be there for a very long time. I always see my work for a client as joint work.

In an interview you once said that being an Israeli, the desire to fuse the Israeli with the European is something you don't like very much …   (laughs) Things change and today my answer would be different. I would say that even if I work in English, I am what I am. I guess I meant to say that I don't like to be trendy in any way. I live inside my research, and sometimes I connect to what is happening out there and sometimes I don't, and that is fine with me. I think that being Israeli or Jewish-born and having all this beautiful tradition such as Hebrew letters as a background is something that makes me who I am. I don't have to adjust to the western way of doing things. I don't have to act like a London-based designer and I don't have less confidence because I am sitting here in Givatayim. I believe that having my own roots will be a great contribution to the world's visual culture. I would like to be a very active protagonist in the world's playground, and in order to achieve that I feel I must be as attentive to my own roots as possible.

But don't you think that working with Hebrew letters might limit your audiences and thus make it harder for you?   Yes and no. I feel that in my early stages, Hebrew was a very strong exception that made people pay attention to my work. But since then, the typographic concepts I have come out with have become stronger and more sophisticated so that I don't insist on Hebrew any longer. My dream is to do typographic work with each and every type system in the world.

Speaking of which… You said that you will escape into the future from what has become mainstream. What are your plans?   Well, you will have to wait for my next book to discover that (laughs).

Experimental Work
How does typography behave in different situations?

by <u>Kitty Bolhöfer</u>

"WHAT DO LETTERS DO WHEN THEY ARE HAPPY?
HOW DO THEY LOOK WHEN THEY ARE SHY?"

∞ When Oded Ezer closes the studio door in his Givatayim home behind him in order to attend to his experimental work, he enters a whole different world. Givatayim – to a non-Israeli the name of this small city on the outskirts of Tel Aviv – sounds like a fairytale place like Middle-earth or Narnia. It sounds like a place where inhabitants are given time – maybe for things other than routine duties and responsibilities: the things for which everyday life does not allow room. Oded uses his 'given time' to escape from the banal, predictable demands of the market he works for as a graphic designer. At night, when he has accomplished his share of commercial work for the day, a business he very much enjoys but that first and foremost helps to pay the bills, the typographer from Givatayim turns into a typo wizard who makes letters come alive. "Playing a game seriously like a six-year-old" is how he puts it, and so his studio becomes a playroom nursery where compromises or rules are not allowed. In his own world, he conceives completely novel approaches to usually anonymous communication tools, realizes and enhances them until sensual, even vulnerable characters arise. Here, letters seem to extricate themselves from the two-dimensional habitat into which the human race has locked them. Oded Ezer allows them to inhabit a new, three-dimensional living space. Some letters become transgenic creatures, crawling out of their sheet of paper; some become unruly, rising up from the page like little kids who refuse to stay in bed, and others even merge with the human body.

What surprises the beholder most about this marvellous work is the degree of scientific accuracy to which Oded fathoms the possibilities of alternation. Through his experiments and studies he tries to find answers to stubborn questions that pop up in his mind: questions of composition, structure, balance, but also of the character's nature. In order to find the answers, he invents very creative and at the same time surprisingly simple methods such as taking a letter, inserting pushpins into its junctions and rotating its limbs just like the arms of a clock. How much turning can the letter bear? At what point of transformation does he lose the letter? Where are the boundaries of legibility and how important is it at all? The documentation of this process becomes an artwork in itself. It is evident that the beauty of his work is based on ingenuity, but the particular Ezer aesthetics that make him stand out from the crowd are also achieved by something that is very refreshing in this computerized era: low tech. Cheap, everyday materials such as matches, chewing gum, sponge, silicone, clay or newspaper pages not only give his letters their own bodies and texture; they also lead Oded to completely different ideas in a way that no state-of-the-art technology ever could. They lead the way to a whole different typographic world inside his playroom nursery in Givatayim.

Experimental Work Oded Ezer

Biotypography The main idea of "Biotypography" is to use biological systems, living organisms or derivatives thereof, to create or modify typographical phenomena. This project deals with manipulated Hebrew and Latin "typo creatures", some sort of new transgenic creature, half insect, half letter. Here, Oded acted as a typographic scientist who cloned ants and implanted typographic information into their DNA. These small typo creatures are made of black polymer clay ("Fimo"), black sponge and plastic. The initial sketches were ideas only, but they changed, developed and eventually became real. "I was seeking to create live, almost cinematic situations where these typo creatures would start to act. The most diffi-cult thing while working on the project was the 'balance' issue – where to draw the line between the insect and the letter.

How recognizable does the ant have to be and how legible should the letter be? It took me some time to understand that I don't really need the whole ant to make my point and that the letters don't necessarily have to be complete. Most interesting were the relationships that were created between the typo creatures when I put them together. When more than one typo creature was present, very surprisingly, a kind of documentary situation, became almost real."

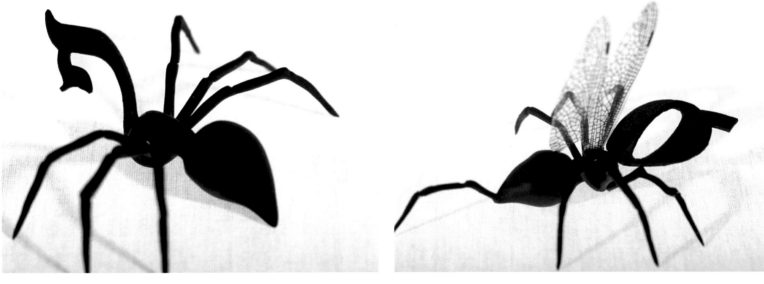

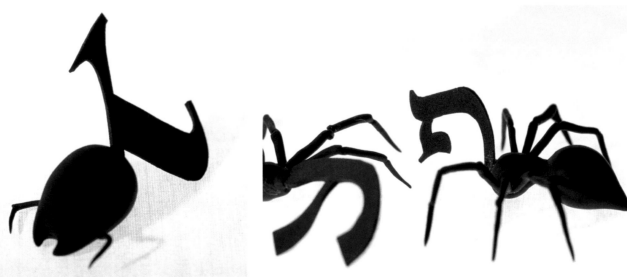

109

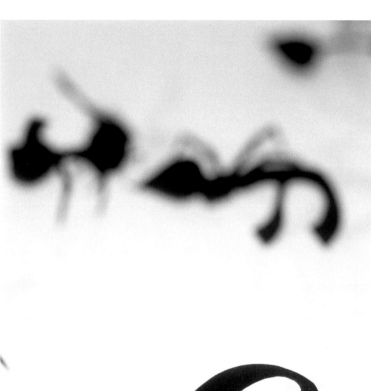

Details from the Biotypography project
Self-produced, 2005 - 2006

Typosperma   Typosperma is the second experimental typo project in Oded's 'Biotypography' series. As a paraphrase on the definition of biotechnology, 'Biotypography' is a term that refers to any typographical application that uses biological systems, living organisms, or derivatives thereof, to create or modify typographical phenomena. The main idea of the 'Typosperma' project was to create some sort of new transgenic creatures, half (human) sperm, half letter. These imaginary creatures are cloned sperms, whose typographic information has been implanted into their DNA.

Oded Ezer as a typo-scientist
2006

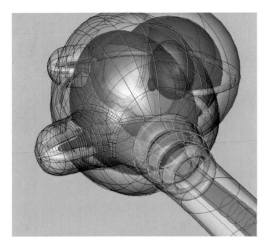

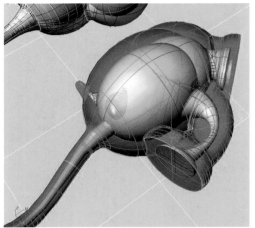

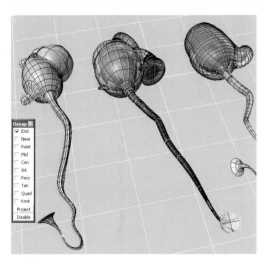

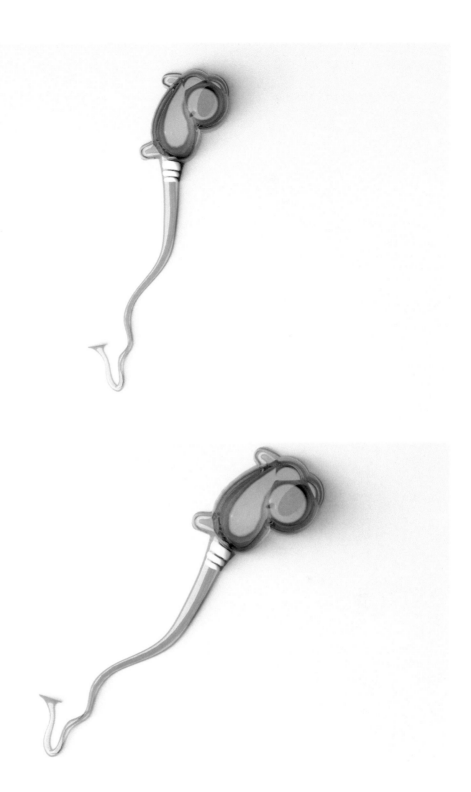

3D rendering process of the Typospermatoids

Experimental Work   Oded Ezer

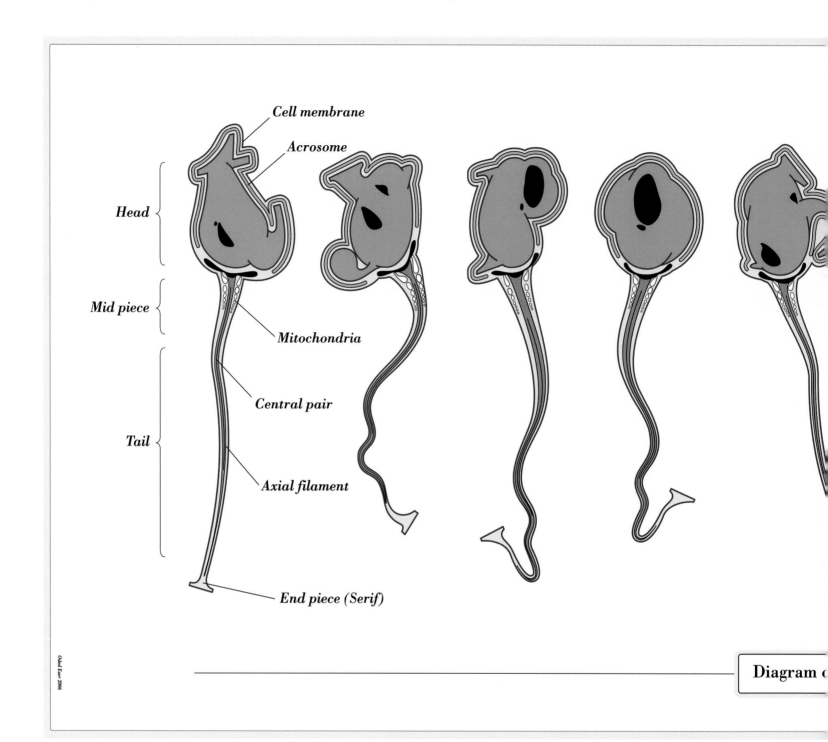

Cell membrane

Acrosome

Head

Mid piece

Mitochondria

Central pair

Tail

Axial filament

End piece (Serif)

Diagram o

Diagram of Human Typosperma
2006

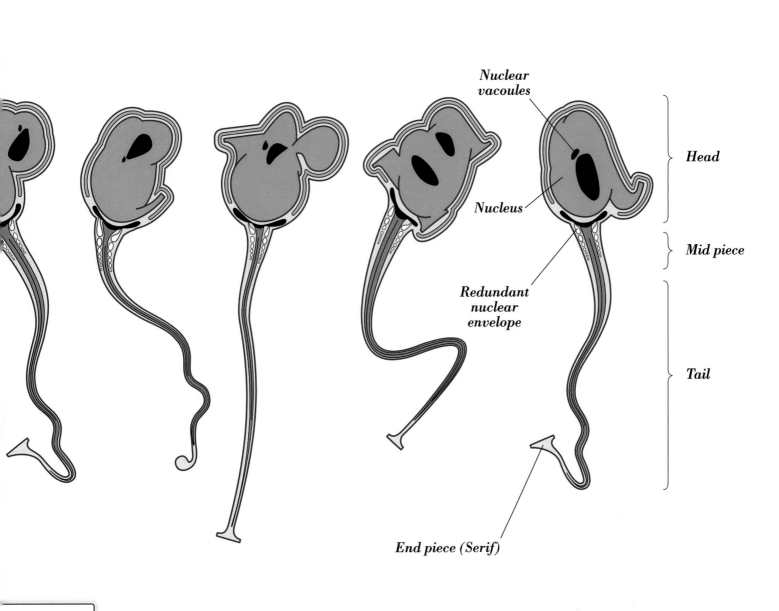

Nuclear
vacoules

Head

Nucleus

Mid piece

Redundant
nuclear
envelope

Tail

End piece (Serif)

posperma

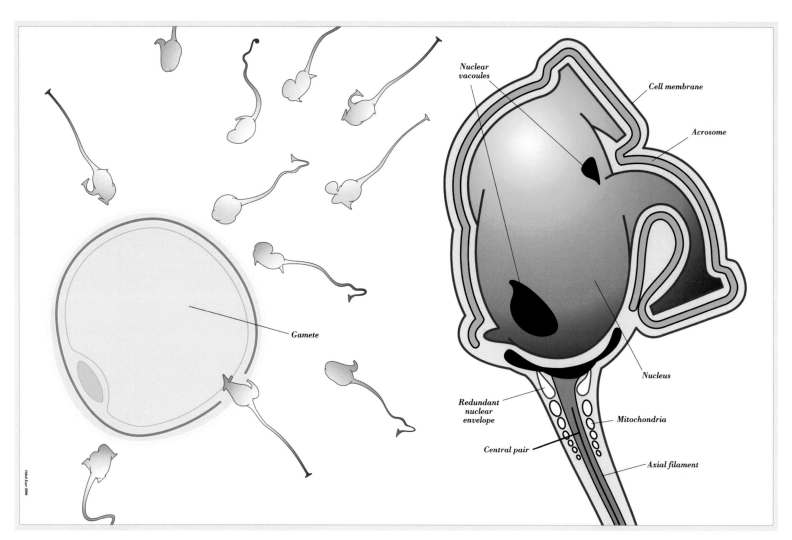

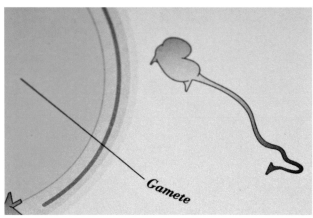

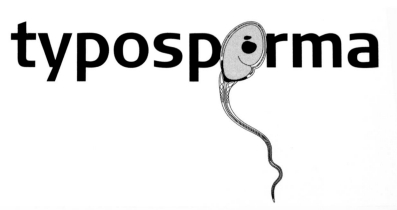

Sketches and diagram details of a Human Typosperma
2005 - 2006

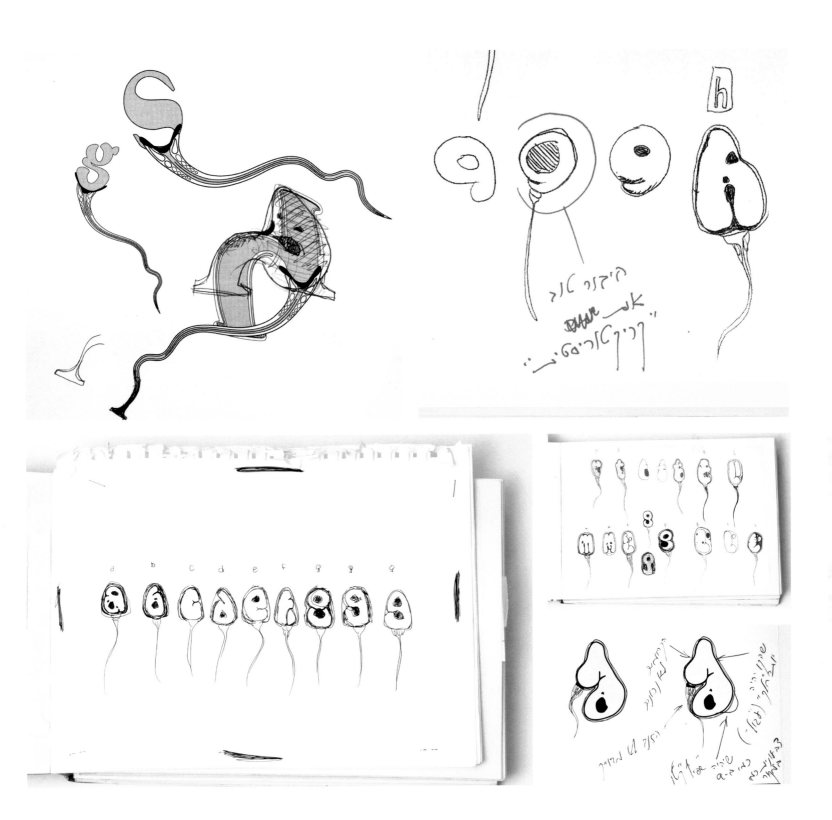

Detail from the Typosperma project
2005 - 2006

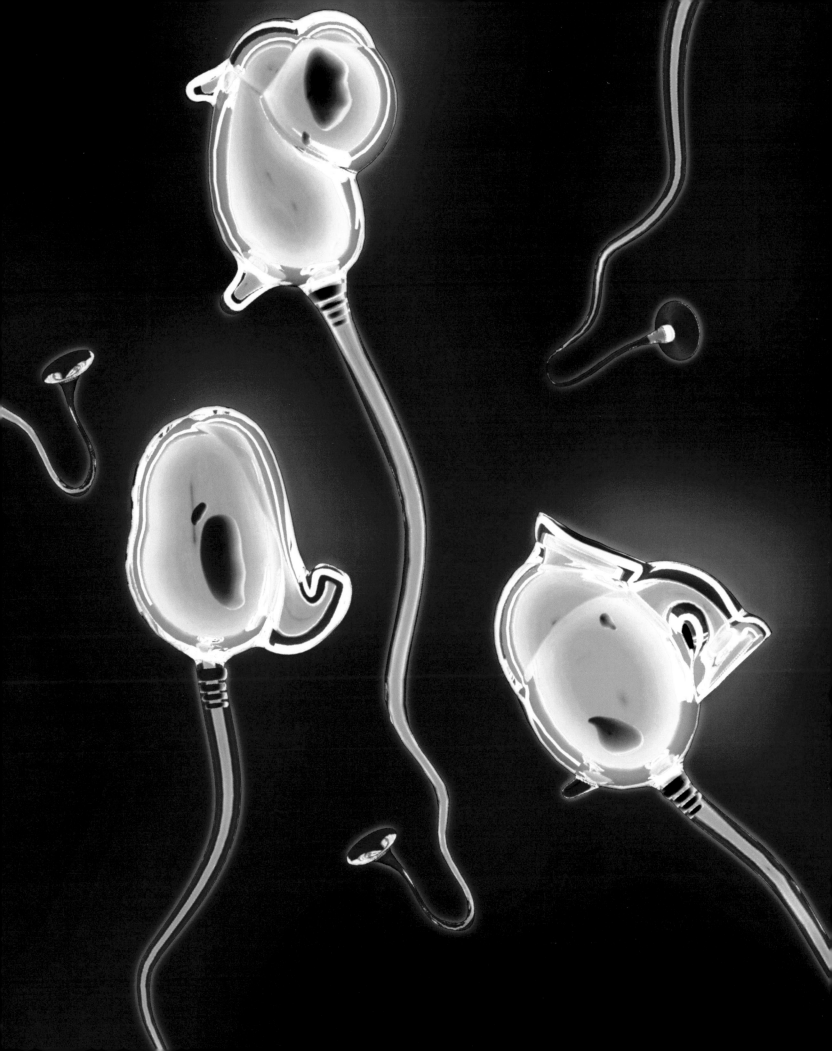

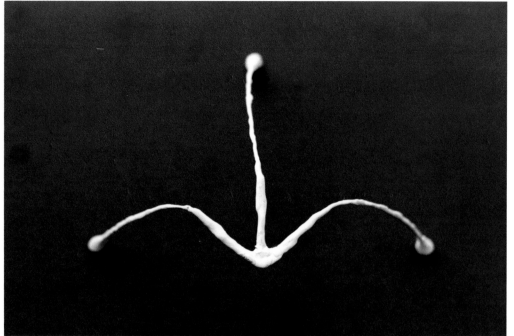

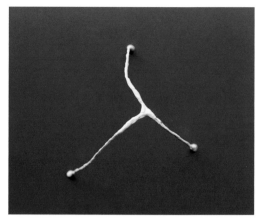

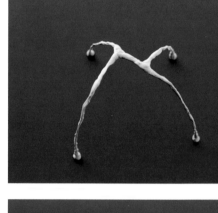

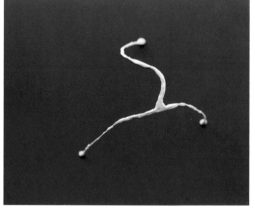

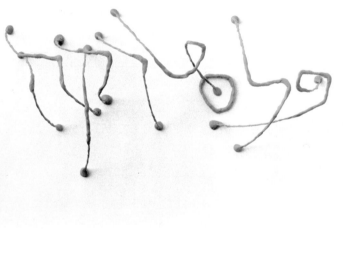

Plastica 3D Hebrew letters
Details

Plastica poster
Manifest for Hebrew type designers
2001

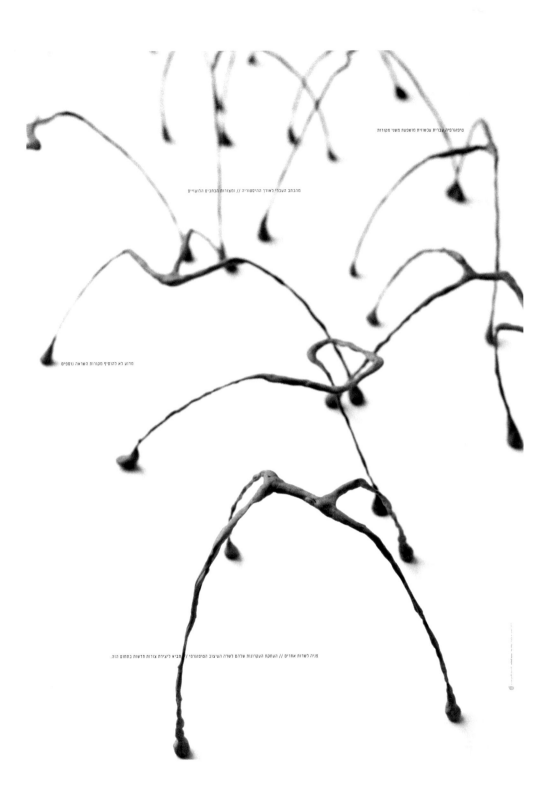

טיפוגרפיה עברית עכשווית מושפעת משני מקורות

מהכתב העברי לאורך ההיסטוריה // ומצורות הכתבים הלועזיים

מדוע לא להוסיף מקורות השראה נוספים

פניה לשדות אחרים // העתקת העקרונות שלהם לשדה העיצוב הטיפוגרפי // תביא ליצירת צורות חדשות בתחום הזה.

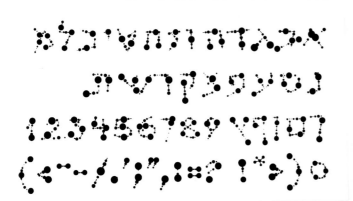
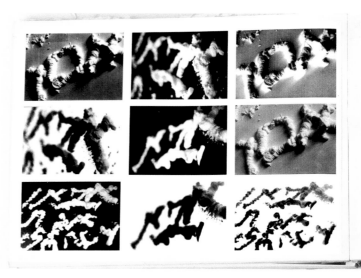
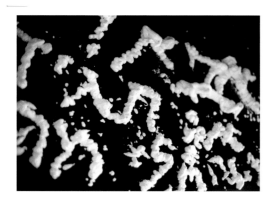

**Details of 2D and 3D studies
made of foam and polystyrene**
2002

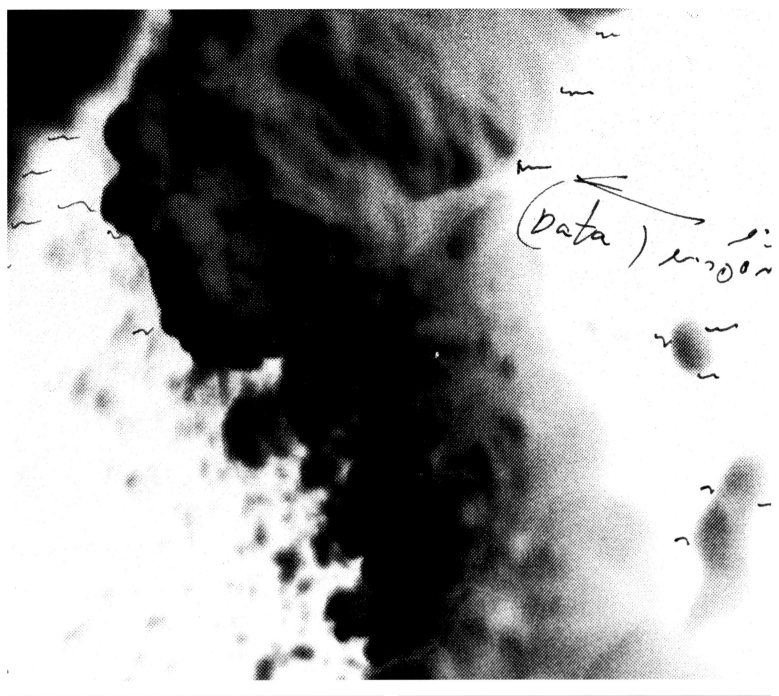

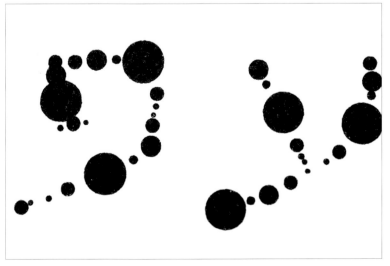

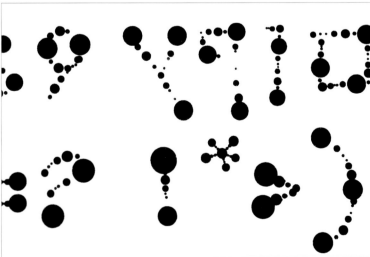

Unimportant & Nothing poster
A typographic homage to
the Israeli poet Yona Volach, 2004

"I love working with low-tech materials such as
nails, glue, foam, silicone etc. I think good design
should be easy to accomplish, so I like simple
ideas and I try to avoid complicated solutions.
This poster is a typographic homage to the Israeli
avant-garde poet Yona Volach, based on a model
made from chewing gum. The inspiration came
from one of her poems called 'Stami Veklumi'
which roughly translates as 'Unimportant & Nothing'. The idea was to create those words from a
confection made uniquely to be chewed, not swal-
lowed; a food with basically no nutritional value. I
had to chew about 10 pieces of gum, one after
the other in order to complete this piece (and it
was absolutely the last time I ever did this)."

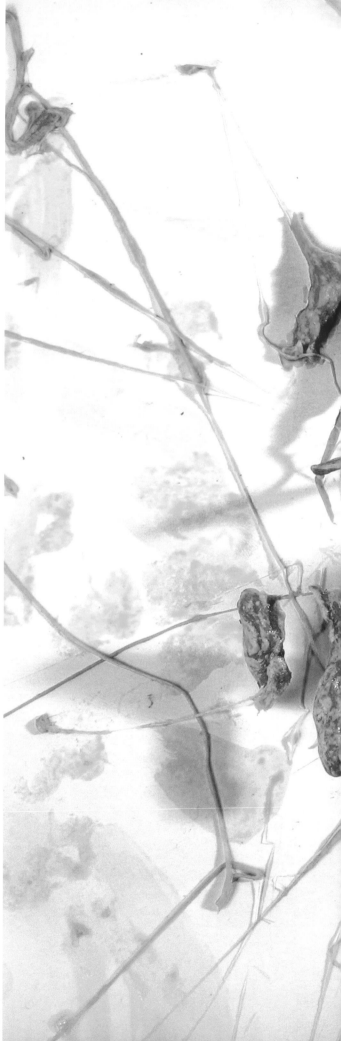

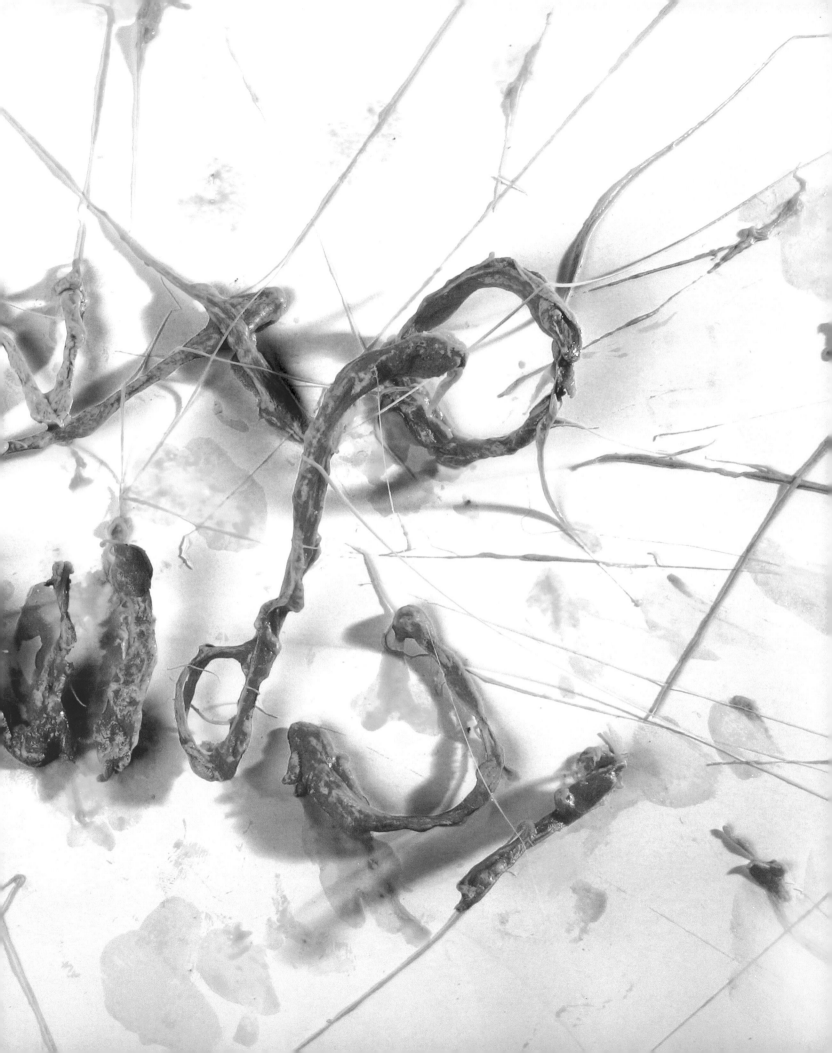

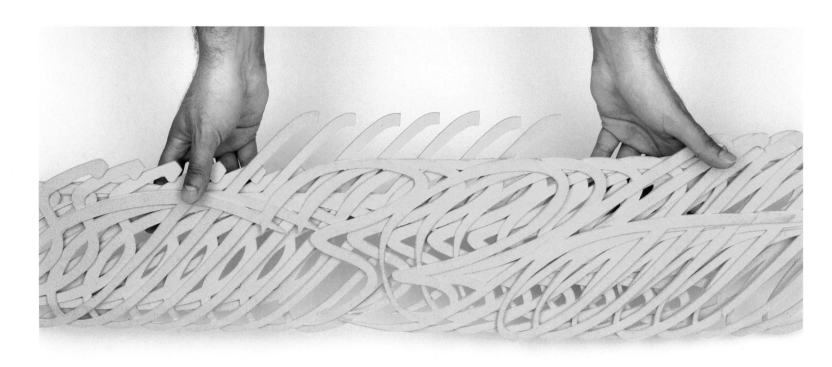

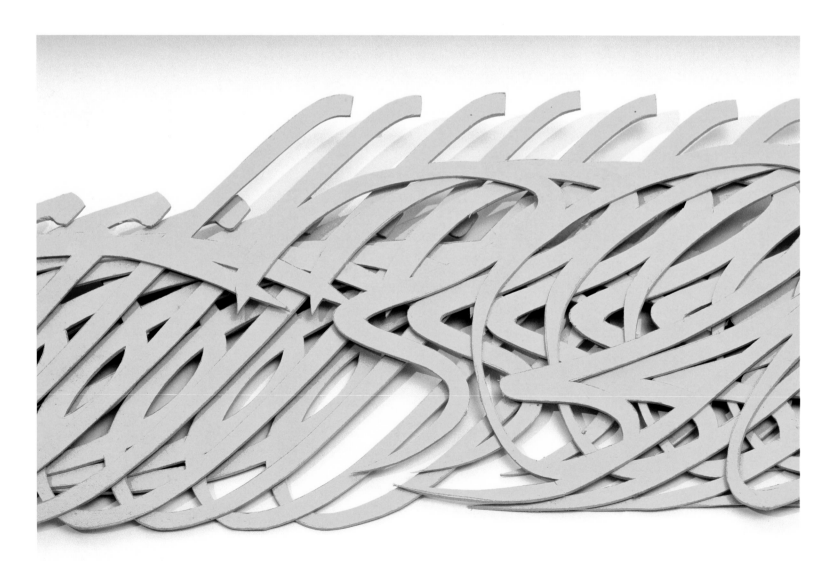

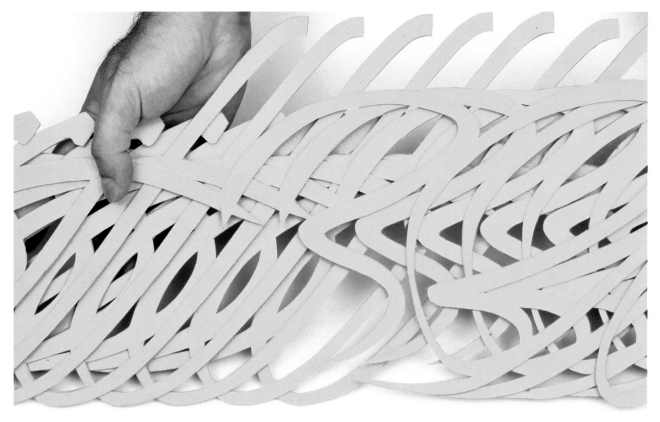

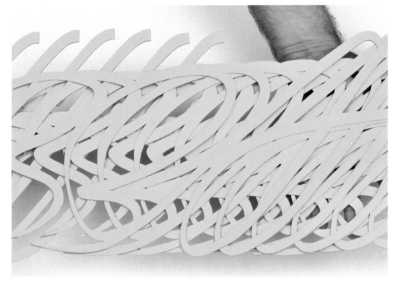

Signature "This piece was a project I did as a student at Bezalel Academy. I took my own signature, enlarged it, cut it out of cardboard several times and layered the parts. This simple technique adds a somewhat animated effect to the signature."

Signature
Self-produced, 2004

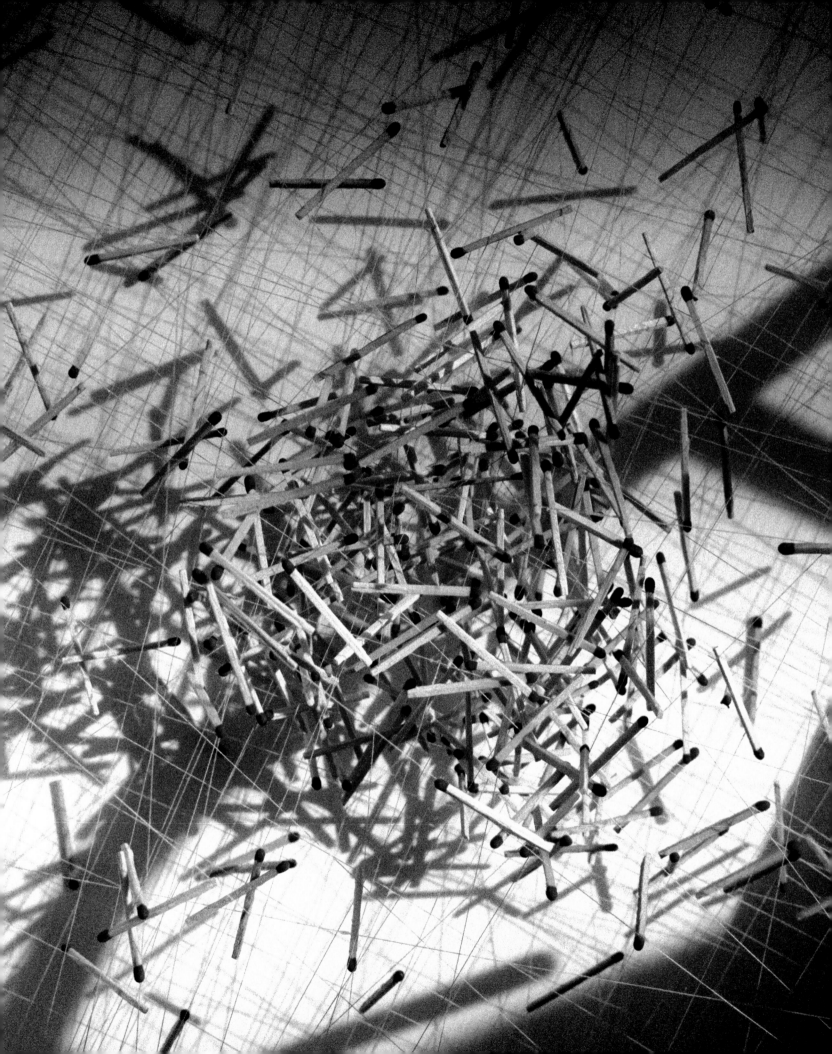

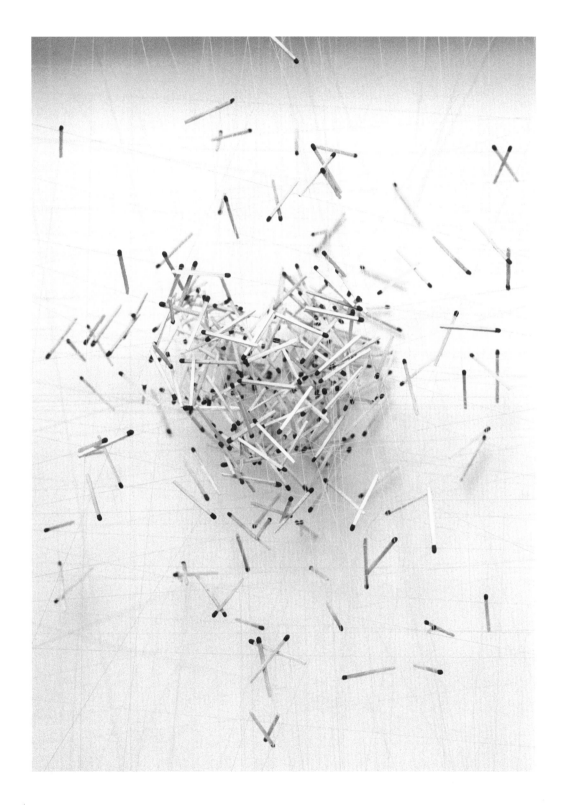

3D Studies
2003

Temporary Type "Temporary Type was inspired by material. In this set, I used old air conditioner filters to give these crumbled letters a special look, as if they were made of ashes or dust.

The game that I was playing here was on the borderline between typography and art. The letters have a meaning, but they are not a medium for direct communication."

Details from Temporary Type project
2006

Oded Ezer

Typo Mythologies "For this project, I dreamt up a story about a tribe in Africa, the last people unveiled to western civilization. Their fathers were aliens from outer space, half letters and half human beings who lived billions of years ago. Once, they sinned against their god, who then punished them by dividing the body from the letter, and that is how humans and language were created. These clay figures are the gods that the tribes pray to."

Typo Mythologies
Details
Clay figurines
2007-2008

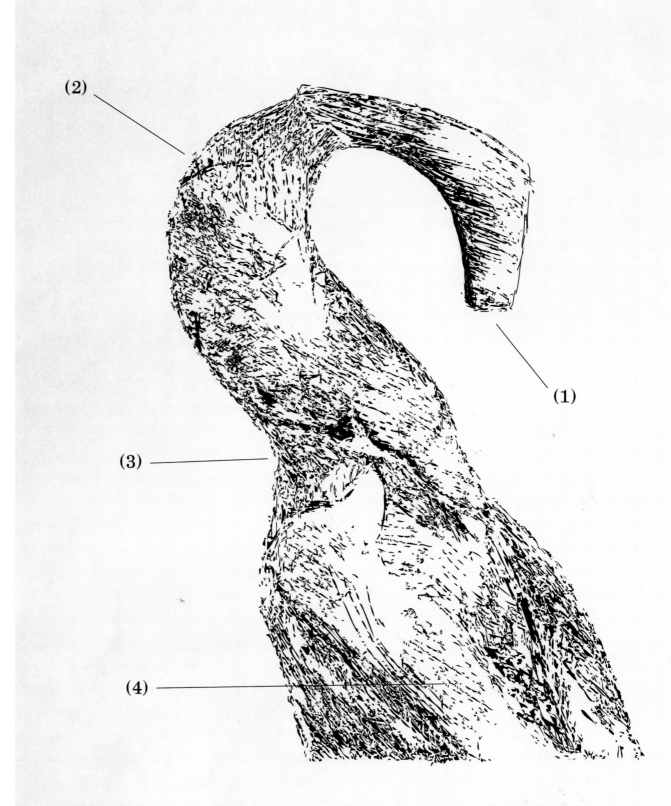

(2)

(1)

(3)

(4)

S-god figurine (Detail)

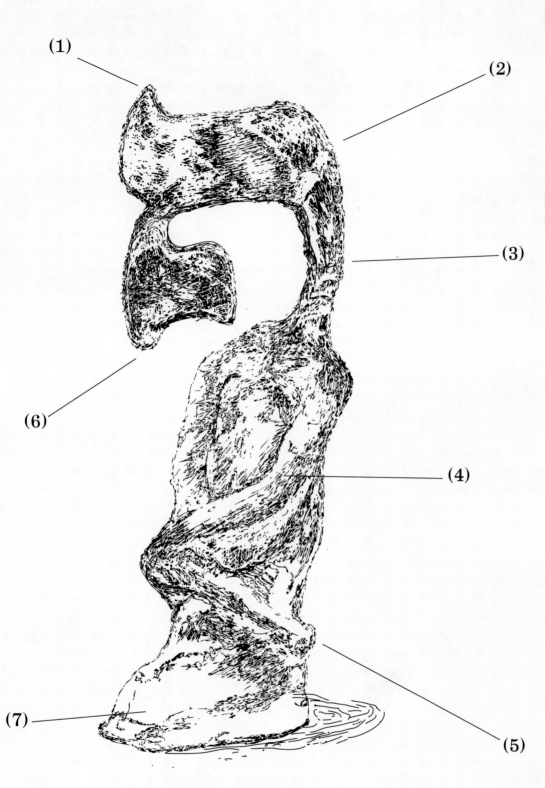

(1)

(2)

(3)

(4)

(5)

(6)

(7)

P-god figurine

The Chorus "I designed this poster for a documentary film named 'The Chorus of the Opera' using my 'Kafka' font. I took a cardboard box which I had found in the trash, pulled strings all over it and hung letters on them as if it was some kind of deserted theatre set. The problem when photographing it was that the small details in the background got lost. After a few unsuccessful tries, I simply put the whole box on a giant scanner and that was it."

The Chorus of the Opera
Poster, 2001

Shalom poster
2005

Declaration of Independence poster
2004

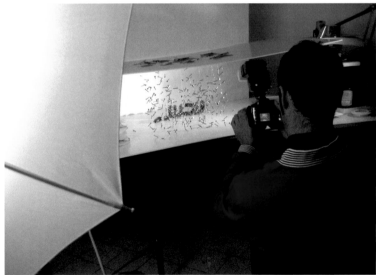

Now This poster is a typographic homage to the work of the Israeli visual communicator David Tartakover. It features the Hebrew word for "now" and is based on Tartakover's 'Peace Now' logo design from 1978.

(Following page) **Now poster**
2004

Rooms "I found these plastic letters in a toy store and used them as a basis for the design. In other rooms, I used black silicone. I just wanted to experiment with large-scale typographical interferences in the surroundings. Because my resources were limited, I couldn't to do it on a large scale; thus I had to use models. On the other hand, you don't know what the 'real' size of a letter is; maybe this already is the real thing."

Details from Rooms Project
2004 - 2005

Experimental Work Oded Ezer

Details from The Rooms Project
2004 - 2005

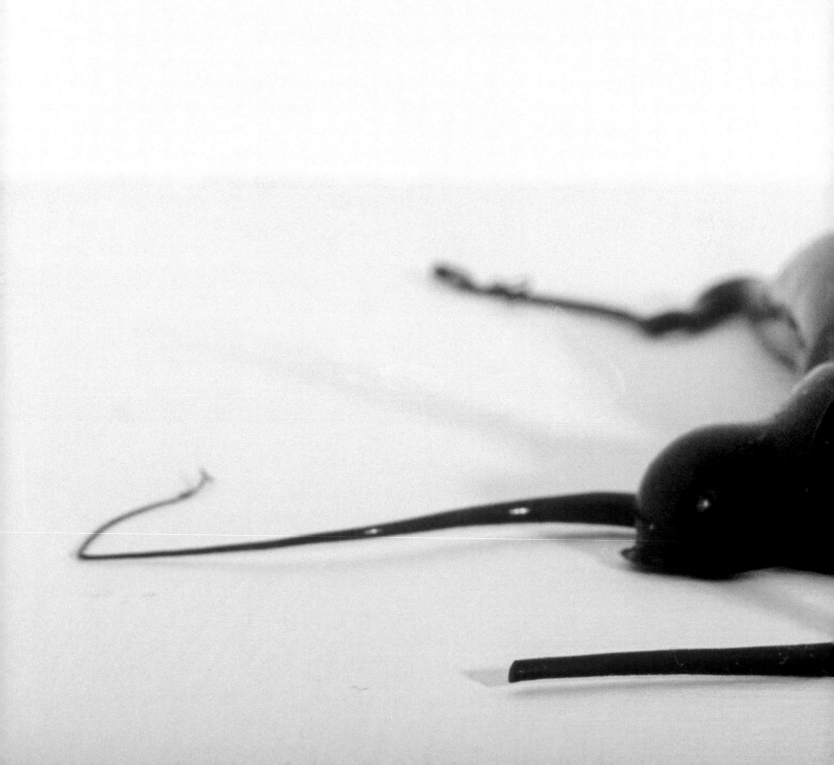

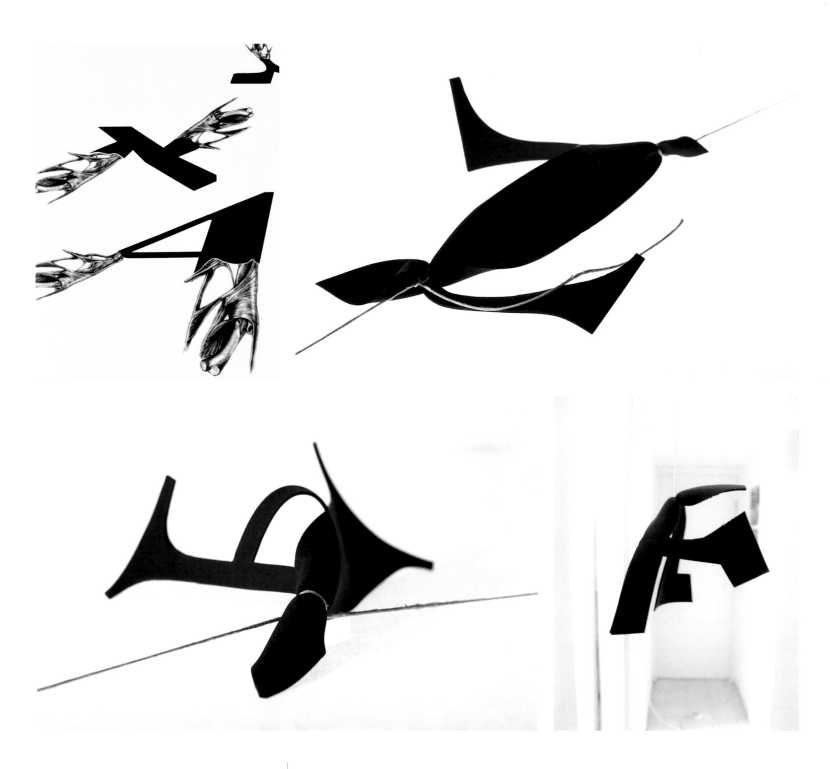

Tortured Letters Made of strings, industrial rubber and wood, the design of the Tortured Letters was inspired by crimes and human nature. Handcrafted elements were incorporated in order to gain authenticity.

Details from Tortured Letters project
2006

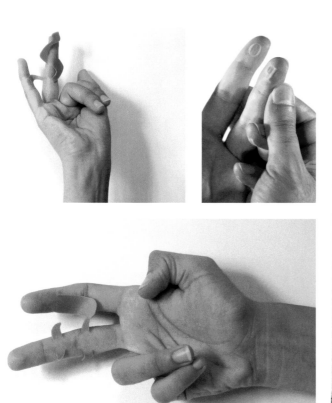

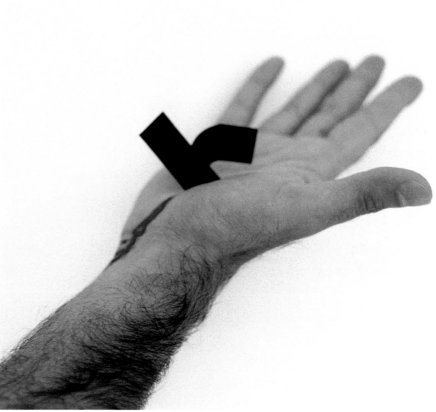

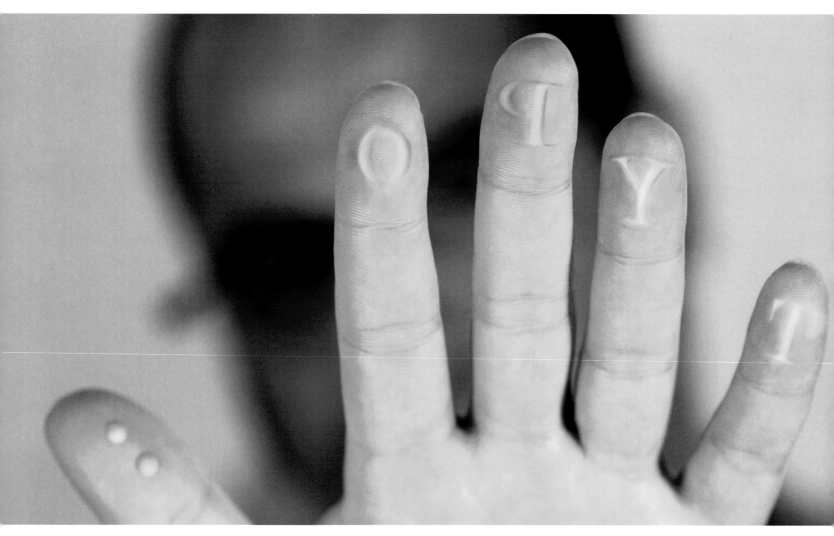

153

Alef poster
A typographic homage to the
'Creation of Adam' painting by Michalangelo
(Alef, the first letter of the Hebrew alphabet)
2003

(Following pages)
Alef 2D and 3D studies
2003 - 2008

a non profit item #9 › oded ezer › a typographic homage to the 'creation of adam' painting by michelangelo › printed in Israel 2003 › עוד עזר › הומאז' טיפוגרפי לציור 'בריאת האדם' של מיכלאנג'לו ›

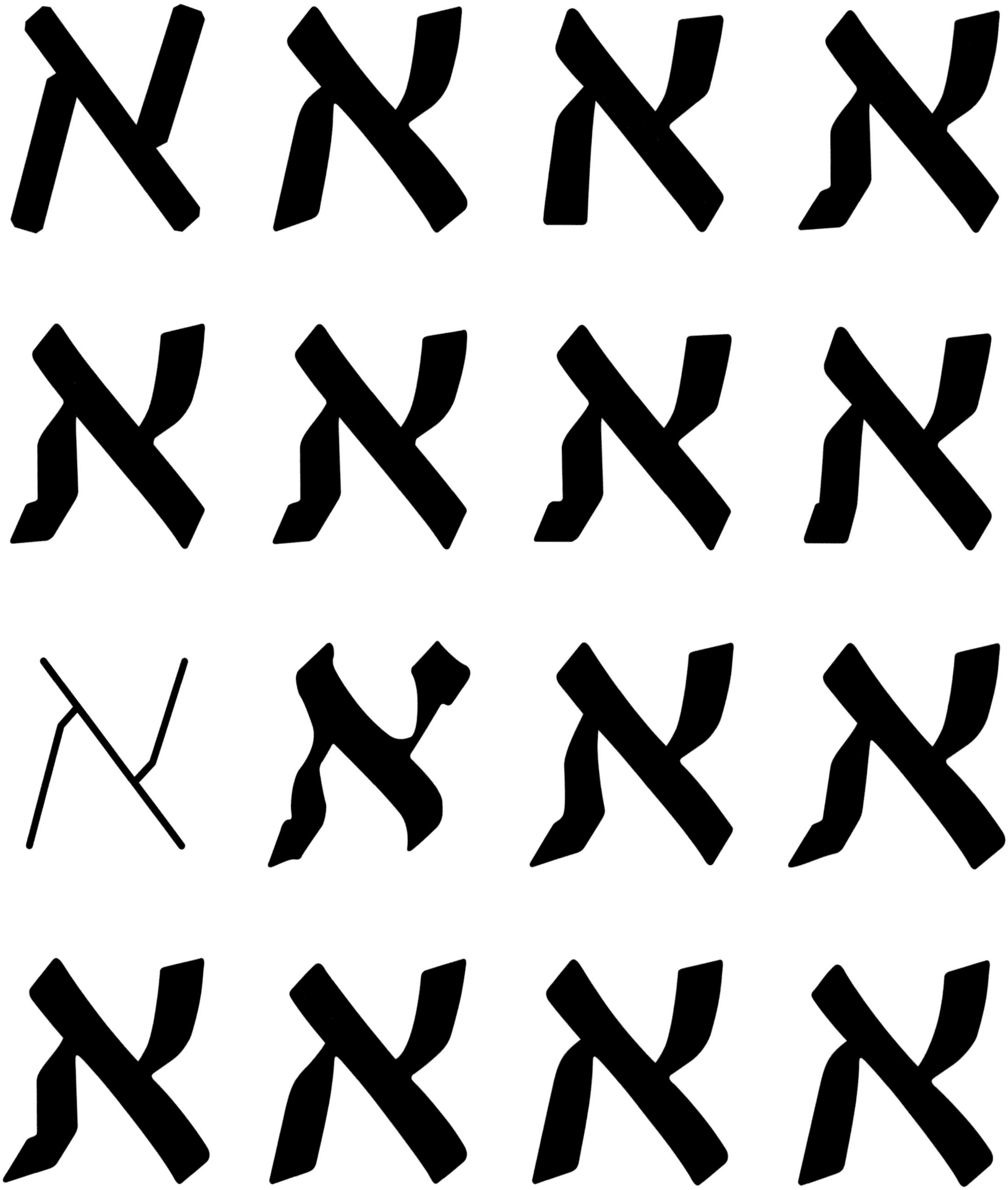

Experimental Work Oded Ezer

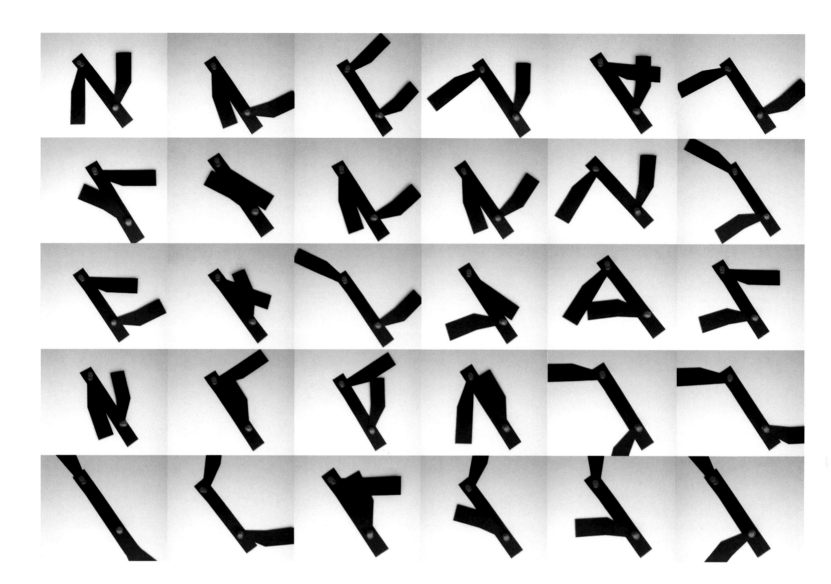

3D Study "Here, the starting point was my own design for the Alef of a typeface called Ta'agid, which is a commercial typeface I sell. Ta'agid means 'corporate' and I called it that because the typeface is very generic. I used its Alef for a study on the structure of a letter. I inserted two push-pins into the two main junctions of the letter and just started playing as with the hands of a clock.

I wanted to find out at what point I lost the Alef. And I noticed that I lost it right away. At one point it even turned into a Latin 'A'. This experiment has led me to the conclusion that if I want my letters to remain legible – at least in some way – I can't change the basic structure too much, but I can make changes on top of the basic structure." **3D Studies**
2003

Experimental Work   Oded Ezer

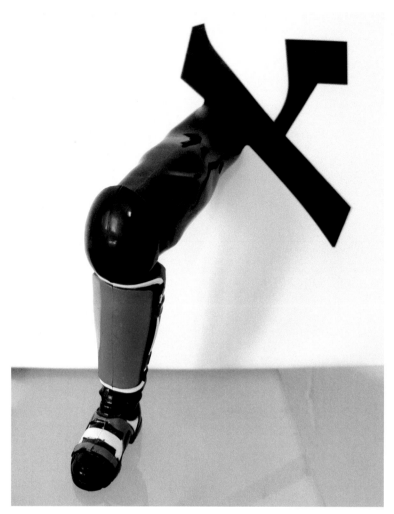 

3D Study
A homage to Marcel Duchamp.
This Dadaist inspired piece of work
is part of the Typrid phase,
combining letters and actual 3D items.

Typographic Fox "The design company 'Studio Shual' asked their friends to create an interpretation of their name, which translates into 'Studio Fox'. Created in cooperation with designer Yaal Tevet, the idea was to make a 'real' Shual out of the word in my Kafka typeface, using computer rendering. This is one of the drafts I made which I actually never turned in."

Typographic Fox
2005

M
A study as part of the "Finger" phase. Letters are lifting themselves off the page.
Oded calls it 3D calligraphy, 2008

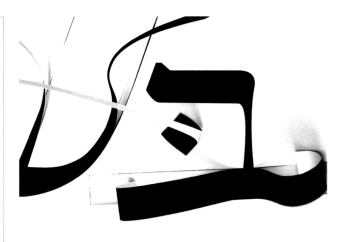

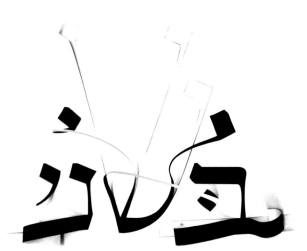

Ketuba
(Jewish marriage agreement)
2007

"On 'Ketuba', I applied the same technique as on 'I love Milton' and 'The Finger'. My aim was to do something beautiful without being kitschy. Most Ketubas, which are prenuptial agreements, are very pretty, but also over the top. I wanted to do something romantic, but without being corny."

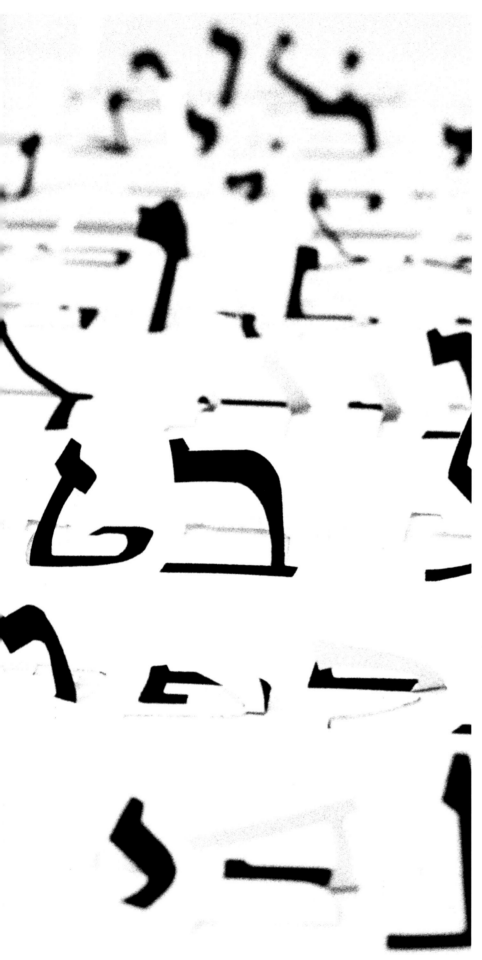

קיבות ללוטן

והזמן כנוצה ווגע

חורביחיר עפלה

שמאל מין

שיר לווי

בחנות הצפרים

גוסל בטרזיינשדאט

בס אלפים

אילנבי אילעבי

The Message
Typographic homage to the music
of the Israeli composer Arie Shapira
2001

___

"I created this model with the names of Arie Shapira's music
pieces simply printed, cut in some parts, and then pulled off
the paper. That was my reaction to his amazing music, which
was hard to listen to, very political and made up of a lot of little
fragments."

The Finger "The Finger" is an imaginary landscape of Hebrew letters. It was originally created as a homage to the Israeli poet, choreographer and art critic Hezi Leskley (1952-1994), echoing the title of his first book, published in 1986.

"The Finger" consists of a short movie and a poster.

The Finger
2008

　　Experimental Work　Oded Ezer

I Love Milton "Coming back from 'Typo Berlin', I realized how few experimental works I had created in English in the past few years. I saw the enthusiasm of the audience when I showed a single piece in English, while the Hebrew ones were undecipherable to most of them.

My decision was to increase the number of English works and I decided to start a series of homages to (non-Israeli) designers whom I admire. The first name that came to my mind was the great Milton Glaser, whose 'I Love NY' logo will never leave my head.. It is simple and direct, and I was sure that it would still be recognizable even if I made it more complicated. The 3D model was photographed by my friend, Idan Gil. I wanted the image to be monumental, mysterious and intensive."

I Love Milton poster
2008

EYAL LERNER presenta
Uno spettacolo di teatro musicale:

SCINTILLE DI GLORIA

Chi scenderà per recuperarne la memoria?

Cura dell'allestimento Eyal Lerner

Musiche di Weill, Stravinskij, Ullman, Zosi, Pärt, Schoenfield

Testi Dalfino, Brecht, Ramuz, Kien, Prager

Interpreti Eyal Lerner (narrazione, canto), Laura Dalfino (soprano)
Marco Ortolani (clarinetto), Alberto Bologni (violino),
Andrea Noferini (violoncello), Giuseppe Bruno (pianoforte)

Scintille di Gloria "I am fascinated by the strong impact of two-dimensional letters that suddenly liberate themselves into space and in doing so, transfer additional conscious and unconscious messages. I was asked to design a typographic poster for a theatre event produced in Italy called 'Sparks of Glory', marking the European day, Jan- uary 27th, for commemorating and honoring the victims of the Holocaust. I made the free endings of the letters turn into threatening barbed wires and used a strong contrast of black and white and a dramatic composition in order to transmit despair and courage."

Scintille di Gloria
2008

Open "I recently made this poster for a brand design company called OPEN T.B.E. It was at the same time I did the 'Finger' poster and I was interested in applying what I had learned to an English word as well. I printed a big OPEN on white paper, and then simply cut out some parts of a magazine cover, put them on top and pulled the edges out - as if they were blowing in the wind, revealing the inside parts of the letters."

Tybrid "Tybrid" consists of 4 squares (each 50×50 cm) combined together, forming the Hebrew word for "Typography". This work was created specially for an invitational poster exhibition themed "My Favorite Game", that was held in July 2007 in Ithaca, and in September that year in Athens, Greece.

"I dealt with formal intersections between traditional Hebrew letters and various object silhouettes, consciously ignoring 'logical' contexts. Using beautiful vector silhouettes from Stefan Gandl's book and the popular Frankrühl Hebrew typeface, I freely and intuitively released myself from ergonomic and functional restrictions, using methods and materials developed in some of my former experimental works. This poster series is also influenced by Dadaist works and contemporary virtual hybridizations of animals and human beings. I have treated this work as a suggestion for typographic, visual expression, something to look at and not necessarily to write with."

Details and documentation of the "Typrid" work process
2007

**Details and documentation of the
"Typrid" work process**
2007

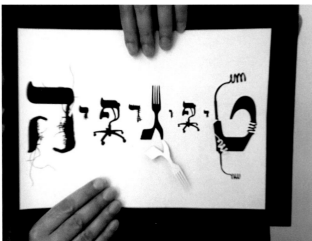

Experimental Work Oded Ezer

Tybrid (1 + 2)
2007

Experimental Work Oded Ezer

Tybrid (3 + 4)
2007

Experimental Work Oded Ezer

Helvetica Live poster
2008

A personal homage to Helvetica. The objects that are con-joined with the letters are silhouettes from Stefan Gandl's book "NeubauWelt" and were chosen intuitively to match each letter individually.

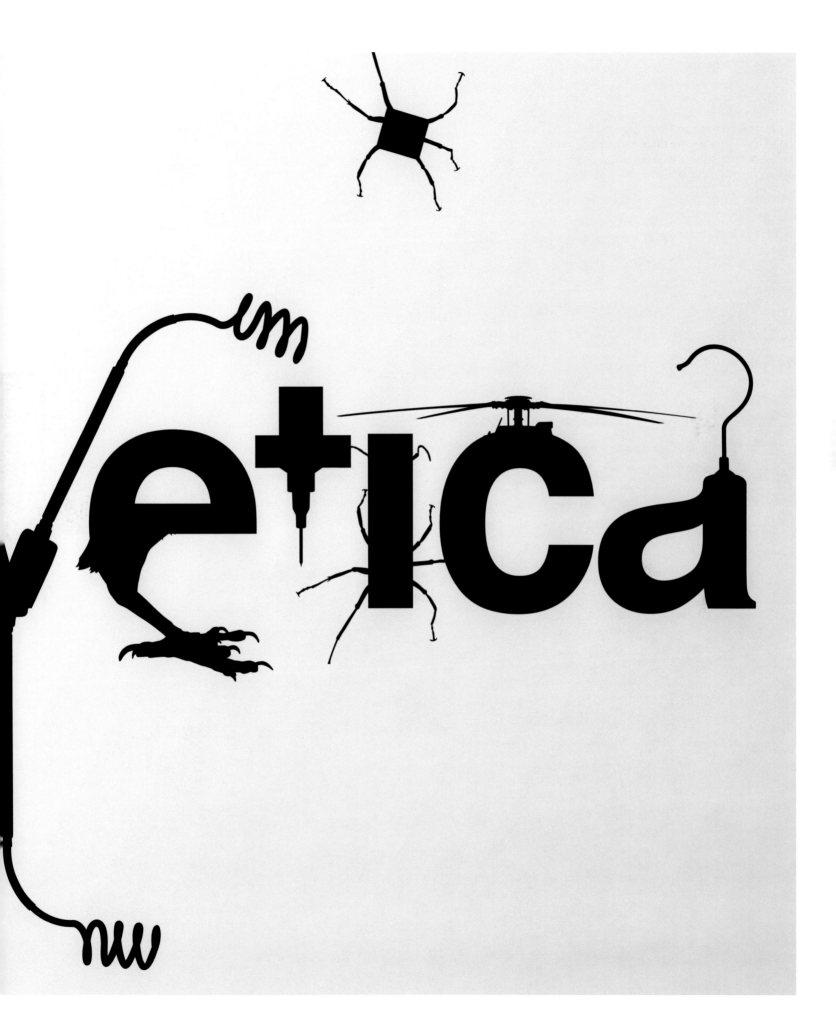

Index

לאדר, בני היקר.

All projects created, art directed
and designed by Oded Ezer
© Oded Ezer Typography
All photos by Oded Ezer,
except when noted differently

FONTS

Frankrühliah / Tipografya
pp.: 016–027
Photos: Idan Gil
Artist portrait: Ruthie Ezer
Frankrühliah notebook
Designed in cooperation with Anat Safran

Greeting Cards
pp.: 042–043
Photos: Idan Gil

NPI logo
pp.: 046–047
Photos: Idan Gil
Artist portrait: Meital Gueta

Typeface design
Photos: Idan Gil
Artist portraits: Salomé, Maya Brill

GRAPHIC WORK
Photos: Idan Gil

CoPro2000
pp.: 052–053
Photos: Amos Rafaeli

ezer!shapes
pp.: 054–055
Photos: Idan Gil

I love Istanbul
pp.: 050–051
Photos: Idan Gil

Sketchbooks
Photos: Idan Gil

EXPERIMENTAL WORK

Biotypography
pp.: 106–111
Photos: Idan Gil
Assisted by Liat Aluf

I Love Milton
pp.: 172–173
Photos: Idan Gil

Ketubah
pp.: 164–165
Artist portrait: Meital Gueta

Political Typo
pp.: 140–143
Photos: Shaxaf Haber ('Now' poster), Idan Gil ('Shalom' poster)
Assisted by Liat Aluf

Rooms
pp.: 144–149
Photos: Idan Gil

Tortured Letters
pp.: 150–151
Photos: Idan Gil, Oded Ezer

Typo Mythologies
pp.: 134–135
Photos: Idan Gil
Artist portrait: Ruthie Ezer
Technical illustration: Ifat Yairi
Assisted by Ruth Pikado

Typoplastic Surgeries
p.: 153
Photos: Idan Gil and Oded Ezer

Typosperma
pp.: 112–119
Photos: Ruthie Ezer
Rendering: Amir Lipsicas
Scientific consultation: Hagit Altman Gueta
Assisted by Ifat Yairi

Unimportant & Nothing
pp.: 126–127
Photos: Shaxaf Haber

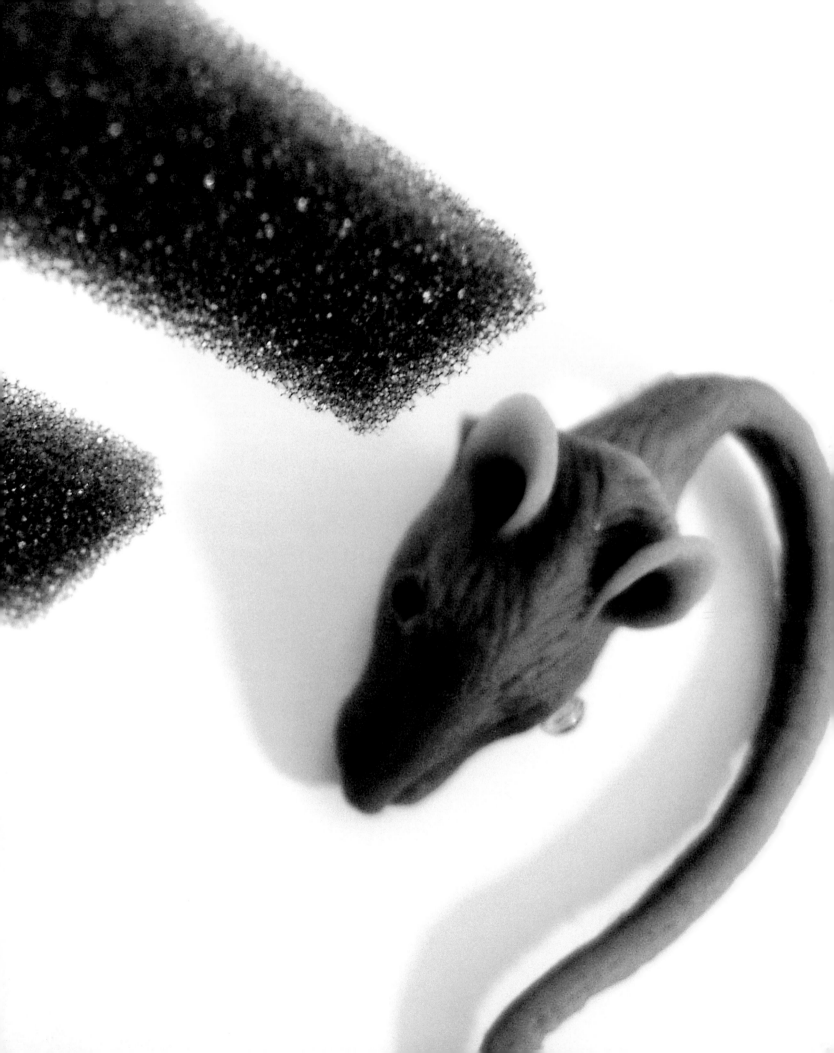

Oded Ezer The Typographer's Guide to the Galaxy

Imprint

Edited by **Robert Klanten**
Forewords by **Paola Antonelli, Marian Bantjes**
Text Editor **Kitty Bolhöfer**
Text features by **Yehuda Hofshi** and **Cinzia Ferrara**

Cover by **Floyd Schulze** for Gestalten
Layout by **Floyd Schulze** and **Hans Baltzer**
for Gestalten
Typeface: Neutral BP by **Kai Bernau**

Project management by **Julian Sorge** for Gestalten
Production management by **Janni Milstrey**
for Gestalten
Production assistance by **Natalie Reed**
for Gestalten
Proofreading by **Joseph Pearson**
Printed in Hong Kong
through Asia Pacific Offset

Published by Gestalten, Berlin 2009
ISBN 978-3-89955-242-3

Respect copyrights, encourage creativity!

For more information, please check www.gestalten.com

Bibliographic information published by the Deutsche
Nationalbibliothek. The Deutsche Nationalbibliothek
lists this publication in the Deutsche Nationalbiblio-
grafie; detailed bibliographic data is available on the
internet at http://dnb.d-nb.de.

This book has been printed on PEFC certified paper
which ensures responsible paper sources in accord-
ance with sustainable forest management.

Gestalten is a climate neutral company and so are our
products. We collaborate with the non-profit carbon
offset provider myclimate (www.myclimate.org) to
neutralize the company's carbon footprint produced
through our worldwide business activities by investing
in projects that reduce CO_2 emissions (www.gestalten.
com/myclimate).